PELICAN BOOKS

A453

THE PSYCHOLOGY OF THINKING

Robert Thomson was born at Croft Spa, and has spent most of his time in the north-east of England. He was educated at the Royal Grammar School at Newcastle upon Tyne, and at University College, Oxford, where he studied modern history but changed to modern philosophy and psychology after five years' war service. In 1949 he joined the staff of Durham University, at first lecturing in philosophy, but since 1955 he has lectured in psychology both in the Durham Colleges and at King's College, Newcastle, in the University of Durham. He is now Senior Lecturer in psychology at Leicester University.

His fields of interest are the psychology of learning, personality study, and philosophical problems, especially those connected with psychology.

In collaboration with his colleagues and friend, Dr W. Sluckin, he has written articles on cybernetics.

CONTENTS

EDITORIAL FOREWORD

'THINKING' is a subject of common interest to philosophers and psychologists; and, of course, to others as well. There are, however few authors who are qualified to deal with both the philosophical and the psychological aspects of the subject, and fewer still who can present both aspects of the subject in plain words.

The author of this book came into psychology from philosophy, but he is one of the few students of philosophy who have made it their business to understand the distinctive problems of the psychologist, and the distinctive methods of the psychologist in tackling his problems.

This book provides the most comprehensive, and the most comprehensible, account—to date—of the major lines of exploration in this field. Some other volumes in this series have treated important aspects of the subject. In *Body and Mind in Western Thought*, Dr Wynn Reeves gives a broad historical account of the development of a framework of ideas within which the contemporary problems of psychology have arisen. Dr Sluckin, in *Minds and Machines*, has given a systematic account of certain contemporary ideas with which any theory of thinking must come to terms.

This volume now provides an exposition and critical discussion of the most important recent pioneering studies in this field – ranging from the exciting new ideas and experiments of the Swiss psychologist, Jean Piaget, to the not less exciting and illuminating ideas of American psychologists such as (to mention only two) N. F. R. Maier and Jerome S. Bruner. Hitherto these ideas and experiments have been in the main a preserve of experts and specialists. Now, in this volume, they are made available, without any sacrifice of scholarship and scientific integrity, to all who, for any reason, have had occasion to think, and to think about their thinking.

C. A. MACE

ACKNOWLEDGEMENTS

I WOULD like to thank Professor C. A. Mace for asking me to write this book and for all his kind and most helpful advice during its preparation.

My thanks are due to several psychologists for their help: Professor J. S. Bruner, of Harvard, read Chapter Four and allowed me to use his book while it was still in manuscript; Professor C. E. Osgood, of Illinois, read Chapter Six and helped me to adapt his theory to the specific needs of my book; Dr McKellar, of Sheffield University, also allowed me to use his book, in connexion with Chapter Ten, before it appeared in print; my friend Henri Tajfel put me in the way of much useful material during the early stages of writing and criticized my ideas on learning; I owe much to his erudition as a psychologist and philosopher; another good friend and colleague, Dr Sluckin, read the entire manuscript and saved me from mistakes through his lucid criticisms; Professor F. V. Smith also gave me the benefit of friendly criticism.

It is evident that I owe much to the writings and lectures of Professor Gilbert Ryle: I hope that in the process of adopting his views I have not blunted or misapplied them.

Finally I wish to thank the publishers and authors who have allowed me to use the materials acknowledged in the text and in the lists of references at the end of each chapter. In particular I wish to thank Professor O. H. Mowrer for allowing me to use his article in Chapter Nine. Dr Randolph Quirk, of the Durham University English School, also helped me greatly with this chapter.

The responsibility for any errors and misconceptions is mine.

R. T.

Durham University, May 1958

CHAPTER ONE

What do we mean by 'Thinking'?

ARISTOTLE selected rationality, the capacity to think, as the defining attribute of Man. Descartes sought to distinguish mind from matter by characterizing the former as 'that which thinks'. It is not surprising that these two philosophers should seize upon one of the most distinctive human capacities in their definitions. It is true that many of the activities involved in human thinking are present lower down the evolutionary scale, particularly among vertebrate animals; but the human animal has developed these activities to such an extent that there is a huge gap between man and the next most intelligent living creature. Thought is not necessarily the most significant psychological function, but no understanding of human behaviour can be complete without some study of the fact that human beings have the capacity to think in ways which no other animal is able to achieve. No psychology can be complete without some attempt to describe and explain what a man does when he is described as 'thinking' – however much certain psychologists emphasize the irrational and unconscious factors in human make-up.

But what is thinking? This might seem a pointless question, since everyone knowns by acquaintance what thinking is from his own first-hand experience of doing it. We all think from time to time. Even if we are not philosophers or scientists we have at least followed an argument put to us by a schoolmaster or preacher. We have sometimes been bright enough to spot a flaw in such an argument and have managed to formulate a cogent objection against it. We have been defeated by chess or bridge problems or have battled with such teasers until we have succeeded in reaching a solution. We know very well how some thinking sticks to the point and moves steadily towards its conclusion while other thinking runs round in circles or drifts off into blind alleys or gets bogged down! Some answers to problems come to us in a flash while, at other times we are confused and befuddled in spite of hard efforts. In brief, we know quite a lot about thinking from our own practical experience of thinking. Why should anybody want to discuss thinking and to ask what thinking is?

Very few people ever think about thinking. It is one thing to practise an activity and quite another thing to stand back and try to observe, describe, and account for that activity. It is one thing to realize that certain activities happen, but quite another thing to take special steps to show precisely what does happen and how it happens in the way it does. Those who have traditionally given descriptions of what a man does who thinks have been the philosophers. They have chiefly relied on their own personal experience as their data, and have usually undertaken the inquiry as part of a larger enterprise – that of understanding the world and Man's knowledge of it. It is only recently that psychologists have tried to find out what happens when we think and what conditions influence our performance by applying the methods of science to this human capacity. In neither philosophy nor psychology have the results of this abstract approach to thought been really successful. But, at least, they have shown that thinking is a much more complicated business than common-sense acquaintance with it might lead one to suppose. There are still plenty of facts to find out and many difficult problems to be faced if we want to understand the nature of thought.

What has been achieved so far is worth the attention of the layman, and ought to prove of some interest to him, since it introduces a number of factors relevant to thought concerning which psychologists have attained some knowledge. The purpose of this book is simply to report the present state of knowledge in that branch of general psychology known as the psychology of thinking and to give some typical samples of the data on which this particular field depends.

What do we mean by 'Thinking'?

AMBIGUITY OF THE CONCEPT OF 'THOUGHT'

We must begin, however, by sorting out the common-sense knowledge which we all have about thinking. This is the surest starting-point for any academic inquiry. Moreover, it is readily accessible, since much of it is embedded in our everyday speech, in the ordinary language we use to describe or refer to thinking.

When we describe a person as 'thinking' it is evident that we are using a highly ambiguous concept. The word or its synonyms mean quite different activities according to the context and manner in which it is used. If you ask the old nursery question 'A penny for your thoughts?' the answer might reveal anything from a wool-gathering day-dream to a complex cogitation concerned with a problem in mathematical analysis. The verb 'to think' has such a wide application that, in its most general use, we never stop thinking throughout our waking moments and even indulge in snatches of thought during sleep. Nevertheless we can distinguish several more particular meanings of the concept. What different kinds of activity does the notion of 'thinking' indicate according to conventional usage?

USES OF THE TERM 'THINKING'

(1) Much of our thinking is what psychologists label 'autistic' thinking: fantasies, day-dreams, the idle flitting from one half-formed notion to another. This sort of activity is regarded as the imaginative expression of underlying wishes, needs, or wants.

(2) In quite a different sense we sometimes use a phrase like 'I am trying to think when I last used my season-ticket'. Here 'thinking' is synonymous with 'remembering'. The attempt to recall what we have perceived or learned in the past is totally different from the wishful-thinking of fantasy. It is prescribed by actual happenings in the past and involves an attempt to describe these accurately.

(3) Between the uncontrolled flow of autistic thoughts and the deliberate attempt at recall comes imaginative thinking. Imagination is distinguished from fantasy in that it is evoked primarily

13

by external sources of stimulation, such as persons, things, and events actually perceived. When we fancy or suppose or imagine happenings (which are not actual events either past or present), our pseudo-happenings have a coherence which is modelled on, and derived from, observations of how things usually happen. Imagining what is possible or feasible is often an essential part in the solution of some real problem. Imagination is closely allied with reasoning.

(4) Sometimes we use the imperative phrase 'Think what you are doing!' Here is a command to take heed or pay attention to the execution of a practical task. Some tasks can be done either carefully or in a slapdash manner: others cannot be done at all unless a worker thinks what he is doing. As Professor Ryle (the distinguished Oxford philosopher) has pointed out, 'thinking what one is doing' when engaged in a practical task such as mountaineering does not involve muttering detailed instructions to oneself as one works. It is rather adopting an attitude or frame of mind. We say of a boxer 'Joe lost the fight because he wasn't thinking what he was doing in the sixth round' and we condemn people for 'thinking of nothing but pleasure'. In each case we are not talking about a person's capacity to reason: instead we are referring to a manner or style of behaviour. We can say, in this use of the term, that a person is thinking when engaged in fighting or climbing.

(5) When a man tells us, in social discourse, 'what he thinks' about politics or religion or the local football team or when he asks us 'What do you think about it?' the word 'think' usually means 'believe'.

Everyone holds a number of beliefs, opinions, or views on a wide variety of topics. Such beliefs are rather like habits; we acquire them like habits uncritically, slipping into them gradually and abandoning them just as easily through subtle social influences. Beliefs are induced in us, or broken down in us, by means of 'propaganda' carried out in newspapers, advertisements, political agitators (professional and amateur), or the preachings and pleadings of our friends. Beliefs are picked up,

like fashions, through the unconscious or half-conscious or deliberate imitation of the example set by some group of people.
We are often unaware of what we really do believe until some
crisis or argument forces us to formulate, acknowledge, and defend our beliefs. Basically, beliefs are tendencies to react, consciously or otherwise, in a consistent manner in specific situations. A statement of a belief expresses what the attitude or
tendency is. 'I don't believe in drinking when you're driving'
expresses a tendency (*a*) to abstain when responsible for a ve-
hicle, (*b*) to disapprove of other people who take alcoholic liquor
when in charge of a car or motor-cycle, etc. We usually hold our
own particular beliefs because of certain experiences in the
past: a man's most fixed beliefs carry the stamp of his personal
history. They are the result of the constant process of adapting
needs to the brute facts of the environment.

In spite of the fact that most beliefs are formed uncritically
(and may therefore be dubbed 'irrational') they can be regarded
from a point of view which is strictly logical. Once formulated in
words some beliefs may be looked at as claims: they profess to
be true or, at least, probable. Not all beliefs, of course, are statements; some express moral judgements or sentiments of loyalty,
or aspirations. But those which are statements claim to be capable
of rational support. Evidence is available for or against a particular belief and the producing and ordering of such evidence
introduces a further meaning of the term 'thinking'. Thinking,
in the sense of attacking or defending a belief, may take several
forms. We may attempt to show that the statement expressing
the belief follows without contradiction from certain premises
which are accepted as true by all involved in the argument. Or
we may collect empirical evidence – appealing to observed facts
and generalizations derived from facts (viz. '75 per cent of this
town voted Labour in 1945') in order to show that these data
lead us to the statement as a consequence. Or we may simply
quote some accepted authority – an expert opinion, a dogma, a
custom, or an order from some official – as the ground of the
belief stated. In other words, reasoning of some kind, however

crude, is required in order to establish the validity or plausibility of a particular belief or opinion. Beliefs may be formed in us as habits are, but they can be tested by the application of external criteria; this testing is a variety of thought.

(6) With this mention of the testing of beliefs, we arrive at the concept of 'thinking' in the sense of 'reasoning', 'reflecting', or 'pondering' – with what the old writers used to call the 'intellect'. This meaning is itself somewhat ambiguous. We are thinking, in the sense of 'reasoning', when we are going over a neat argument which has already been worked out and accepted on a previous occasion. Other thinking may involve some kind of work or effort, but there are many different kinds of task which thinkers undertake: mathematical analysis, translating Italian into English, composing music, planning a new department in an industrial firm, designing a hospital building, writing a sermon or metaphysical treatise – besides all the work involved in the physical sciences, history – or the ponderings and calculations of the young man wanting to buy a house for his family. Some intellectual exercises involve the formation of hypotheses in terms of which a range of events can be explained. Other exercises merely require the re-formulation of a practical problem or the definition of a specific topic.

As Ryle has suggested, 'thinking', even in this sixth sense, is highly ambiguous in meaning. The term is what he calls a 'polymorphous' concept. Some concepts such as 'digesting' or 'counting' can be analysed in terms of ingredient processes which always recur in a regular pattern in any activity described by these concepts. But polymorphous concepts are different from these: 'farming' is a polymorphous concept which stands for any one or any set of the quite different doings of farmers. Some farming involves buying and selling cattle: but there are some farmers who do not deal in cattle at all. Ploughing, reaping, hedging, ditching, and milking are all farm jobs; but A and B might both be farmers without having many tasks in common or might perform whatever tasks were common to both their farms in entirely different ways. (The ploughing of a peasant in

India has something in common with ploughing on the corn lands of Kansas; anyone who wanted to find out how different the two situations of the Indian peasant and American farmer turn out to be could probably do so by working for a spell with each!) Now, according to Ryle, the term 'thinking' is, like the term 'farming', a polymorphous concept. Thinkers indulge in many different sorts of work, many different kinds of activity, which have little in common with each other. Two thinkers may live very different lives and have very different capacities, skills, interests, and projects (take the familiar case – the literary scholar as contrasted with the scientist). Furthermore, there need be nothing going on in one type of thinking such that it *must* be going on in any other sort of thinking. The conclusion to which this analysis of the term 'thinking' leads is that if one wants to study what a man does who is described as thinking, in this sixth sense of the word, it is necessary to sort out typical cases and select some of these for special scrutiny. The psychologist in trying to study 'reasoning' or 'reflective thought' is not studying a straightforward process like 'respiration' or 'digestion' or 'sleeping', but must select most or some of a number of different types or species of activity each of which is properly describable as 'thinking' or 'reasoning'.

Yet, in spite of their differences, it is likely that there is some common attribute or set of attributes in virtue of which this particular activity or that may be called 'thinking'. It may be that 'thought' is a disjunctive as well as a polymorphous concept. 'x' is a disjunctive concept if any value has the attribute 'a' OR the attribute 'b' OR the attribute 'c', etc., etc. So that x_1 has a and is therefore categorized as an 'x'; x_2 has 'b' and is therefore categorized as an 'x'; x_3 has 'c', x_4 has 'd', etc. We can, at least, select a number of instances of the category and study each of them in turn.

REFLECTIVE THINKING

When a person thinks reflectively he may do any one or any number of several different things in the course of his thought.

Now whatever differences and diversities, among the recognizable parts of a thought process, may be sorted out by a philosopher, he will agree that there is one thing they all have in common. They are all activities – behaviour patterns which are either overt and publicly observable or else covert yet capable of being objectified under certain favourable conditions.

Consider the case of a thinker at work. How do we describe what he does as he works? We tell the story of his activities. He may work through a series of calculations (using a slide-rule or a calculating machine), discover errors in his formulae, and correct them. He may have an intuition that a particular conclusion is the one he is striving for and then construct a chain of inferences to deduce this conclusion from well-established premises. He may ask himself specific questions and give answers in the light of facts or theories known and remembered by him. He may argue a case – taking first one and then the opposite side in the issue; he may cross-question himself – playing the roles of 'witness' and 'counsel'. During all this he may work it all out in his head, or he may utter his thoughts out aloud to himself or he may jot them down in writing. He may consult books, papers, and mathematical tables in order to complete an inference. Whether he thinks in his head or utters his thoughts aloud or has his thinking tracked by a horribly ingenious machine, a description of his moves and counter-moves and his characteristic intellectual operations can be supplied.

What would this description amount to if it could be obtained with perfect accuracy? Whatever the details, it would be different for each individual thinker. As he 'racked his brains' for the right phrase or hypothesis, as he 'weighed' evidence, as he tussled with a thorny dilemma – we would recognize similarities to other individual efforts, but might also notice highly personal and idiosyncratic features of any particular thinking session.

However, two points may be made.

(1) In the first place, everything that went on would be recognizable as an instance of some familiar kind of activity: calculating, comparing alternative hypotheses and applying various

operations in relation to them, asking questions, giving answers, discriminating discrepancies, etc. From all of which thinking might be characterized as a dispositional concept. It refers, in abstract fashion, to a number of unspecified capacities or skills to carry out certain performances in response to an appropriate stimulus-situation. Thinking, as Professor Ryle has argued with such ingenuity and vigour, is *not* some mysterious shadow-process which goes on behind the overt performances and the strivings of the thinker. 'Thinking', in the sense of 'reasoning' or 'cogitating', is essentially a performance or activity: something which human beings do and which consists in the exercise of capabilities and skills in a special way. What kind of performance precisely, involving what particular skills, and executed in what manner or style, depends upon the context; each individual working at a given time and place and within a particular situation will behave according to the factors involved.

Thought is a variety of dispositional behaviour: as Ryle puts it, very much a matter of 'drills and skills'.

All such thinking is motivated towards a particular goal, and is determined by previous learning and experience. Much of it may be symbolic (using words, images, asking oneself questions in silent soliloquy), but other parts of it are more clearly action (scribbling notes, referring to books, working slide-rules, etc.).

(2) If we want to study the thinking of an individual and especially if we want to compare his thinking with that of other people, we need not take note of everything he does. Ryle has a good example of how this is so. He gives us the illustration of a soldier being questioned about a battle. If the soldier is asked to report on the battle in which he has been taking part, his questioners do not want to be told all the petty details of which the battle and the battlefield actually happened to consist. Nobody wants to know that the sergeant had a quick smoke while consulting a map or that two butterflies flew over the field guns or that there were cowslips in the meadows over which the infantry advanced. Nor is it necessary to know how many bullets were used or how much the uniforms cost. What is wanted is an

account which misses out the details but which gives the important moves and counter-moves, the tactics adopted by each side, and the way in which the battle went. How did it go and why did it go in that way? The account of a battle is an abstract account: it is told in terms which apply to *any* battle, but which when handled in a particular way show how *this* battle went.

Since thinking can be regarded as a disposition – a complex coordination and integration of specific activities – the description of a thought process may be likened to the account of a battle. What moves and counter-moves did the thinker make? What tactics did he adopt, and how did he modify them in the light of obstacles, contingencies, and requirements imposed upon him by the situation? What method of attack did he employ, and what were the results of his strivings?

Although no two individuals may behave in precisely the same way – just as no two battles may follow precisely the same course or include exactly similar incidents – nevertheless when one looks, not at the details, but at the general patterns and outcome, then it is possible to study human thinking abstractly.

At first sight there seems no way of reducing the diversity and complexity of this capacity of thinking to order. But it is not the idiosyncratic features of any stretch of thinking that matters for the psychologist. There are typical operations and systems or groups of operations examples of which can be recognized in any thought process. The ways in which these are evoked and function to produce certain results are the data for any description of 'what happens when a man thinks'.

THE TASK OF EXPERIMENTAL PSYCHOLOGY

When the psychologist deals with reflective thinking he has the following problems:

(1) He must discover what are the typical situations to which subjects respond by engaging in activities describable as 'thinking'.

(2) He must devise a means of objectifying the behaviour of the

subjects he is studying so that a description is possible regarding what happens. The conditions of observation and control must correspond as closely as possible to those of scientific experiment.

'What happens', in this context, means:

(*a*) What operations or groups of operation occur? (What sorts of activity?)

(*b*) What requirements, obstacles, and contingencies does the subject have to meet?

(*c*) What strategies or patterns govern the subject's activities?

(3) The situation must be under some degree of control by the psychologist so that by deliberately varying the conditions under which the subject works, the factors which influence his behaviour can be discovered. What are the variables which, if changed while all other factors remain constant, produce marked changes in the thinker's behaviour?

In other words, the psychologist must devise tests or experiments in which his subjects are required to 'think' and in which they can be observed and the factors involved in the situation isolated for scrutiny. This is a tall order. So far only certain isolated factors which enter into thought processes have been studied scientifically. But nothing less will do — otherwise there can be no psychology of thought; only a common-sense theory about it.

The psychologist is interested in describing what people actually do when they are thinking and what conditions determine the precise patterns of their performance. His job is to discover the facts and explain them: to arrive at empirically established generalizations about thinking and to relate them to other generalizations about human behaviour and to each other in some kind of explanatory system. His job in relation to 'thinking' is different from that of the philosopher. Philosophers are interested in analysing and interpreting the various kinds of knowledge and belief which we have about the world – whether derived from common-sense experience or from scientific research. The philosopher therefore interprets what we know or claim to know about our minds, but it is not his business to find out what as a matter of fact generally happens and how it happens in the way that it does. The philosopher may criticize and evaluate the results of psychological researches, but he does not himself undertake such researches.

THE SCOPE OF THIS BOOK

In this book we are going to be concerned with what psychologists have done in trying to find out what happens when a human being thinks, and how it is that he exercises this capacity in the way he does. 'Thinking' will be taken in the sixth and final meaning which was reached above, namely *reasoning* or *reflective thinking*. Other senses of the term will only be considered in so far as they illuminate the human capacity to reason.

The scope of our discussion will also be limited in various other ways.

Firstly, there are two lines of attack in experimental psychology. The object of psychological study is behaviour, what a living thing does. Now behaviour may be studied by one or other of two methods: mechanistically or behaviourally.

In the mechanistic approach the chief data under scrutiny are the structure and internal properties of the organism itself. The stimuli and the responses made are not so much the subject of interest as are the character of the system (within the organism) which connects stimulus with response and vice versa. In human subjects this approach is that of physiological psychology, which concentrates on the role of the brain and nervous system in guiding behaviour.

The behavioural approach ignores the inner constituents of this nervous system and its internal relations. Attention is focused on what happens when the system as a whole responds to some specific stimulus. For example, an electric shock is administered and the animal which receives it withdraws its limb. The shock is then paired with the sounding of a buzzer. In time the sounding of the buzzer will produce the withdrawal of the limb without the shock being administered. Here the 'stimulus' and the 'response' and their relations to each other are all relatively discrete and easily observed. The reactions of the brain and nervous system are completely ignored, although they unquestionably play an important part in the whole process. This is the approach of experimental and comparative psychology proper.

Psychologists like to coordinate the two approaches whenever possible, giving both a general and a physiological description of behaviour.

However, in this book we shall ignore the mechanical approach. This is not to deny the importance of this approach. But there is little enough information about the working of the brain during thinking and too much space would have to be given to an account of the background of biological and neurophysiological knowledge, necessary to present the neurophysiology of thought processes.

Secondly, how are we to deal with behaviour in thinking? Clearly overt behaviour – what a person or animal can be observed to do in specific contexts – can be defined with reasonable work-a-day precision. But what about covert doings? There are many covert operations in thinking – imagery, unuttered words, tensions, intuitions, impulses, which make their presence felt to the subject but which only he can know and report. These are as important as the overt activities. How does the psychologist deal with these? This raises the greatest of problems in psychology. The psychologist before he begins to theorize must get at his facts, and these are often inaccessible, intractable, and elusive, as well as being extremely complex. Half the battle in psychology is devising a means of getting human or animal subjects to objectify their main activities in such a way that what is really essential in their behaviour can be studied by the psychologist. Quite apart from the difficulty of getting subjects to behave 'naturally' in the course of a psychological investigation, there is the difficulty of getting what is significant in behaviour to exhibit itself clearly. The question which the layman, quite rightly, asks is: 'Can the psychologist really get at the essential facts? Does he perhaps miss subtle elusive factors or fix his researches (unconsciously, of course) so that they confirm his favourite theory?' The answer is that the psychologist is aware of the difficulties and current limitations of his methods. But he would reply that there is no alternative to psychological research and that in the brief eighty years since scientific psychology began there has been sufficient progress to warrant his continuing to plod on. The results of psychology may be limited, but even in our present situation they are often sounder than the opinions frequently expressed on psychological topics by the learned amateur on the basis of his own personal and limited experience. Psychological activities are subject, at least, to criticism and correction both by pyschologists and by philosophers and scientists working in adjacent fields; there is an exchange of information and ideas within the group. Unfortunately many people take it for granted that they know as much as anybody can about human psychology and refuse to regard psychology with an unprejudiced eye. It is noticeable how readily such persons are to adopt any bit of psychological literature (taken out of context) and use it if it supports some part of their own *a priori* theory.

THE PSYCHOLOGICAL APPROACH

In attempting to collect, describe, analyse, and explain the facts of human and animal behaviour the psychologist at present employs several different approaches.

Experiment. The behaviour of actual subjects is sometimes studied in the laboratory under strictly controlled conditions. The situation is organized so that it is simple enough for both stimulus and response factors and the precise manner of their relationship to be observed. The variables which influence changes in the situation ought to be varied one or two at a time, everything else being kept constant, and the data quantified if at all possible. This is roughly the application of the methods devised in the physical sciences to psychological data. Not every psychological function is able to be studied satisfactorily in the laboratory.

Clinical Data. Physicians and clinical psychologists working in hospitals and clinics frequently come across psychological data in the course of diagnosis and treatment of patients, e.g. the behaviour of brain-damaged patients, the data from psychiatric case histories, the investigations into problem children.

Social Survey. The techniques of the interview, the questionnaire, or 'Mass-Observation' study can be adopted by psychologists. This sort of method does not work so well with reasoning as with other psychological functions, although the study of concept formation in children depends upon interviews, cross questionings, etc.

Psychological Tests. The psychological test yields a certain amount of information about the factors involved in thinking and their operational availability in testing-situations.

Introspection and Self-Knowledge. Although liable to error, one can get considerable stimulus from observing something of one's own reactions and those of one's family and friends.

These are several channels through which information can be obtained about what happens in thought activities. But how does one attack one's sources? What do we want to find out? We know where to look and what sort of data to look for, but what sort of question is to be answered concerning this subject matter? What aspect of thinking has to be examined first?

PROBLEM-SOLVING

Examples have already been given of the kind of activity which a man engages in when he is described as 'thinking reflectively'. These activities might be defined as the attempt to solve a problem. John Dewey, sometime Professor of Psychology at Columbia University, pointed out in his book *How We Think* that usually we do *not* think as long as things run along smoothly for us. Habit, impulse, mood, and the well-practised skills of routine help us to drift through much work and play. It is only when the routine is disrupted by the intrusion of a difficulty, obstacle, or challenge that we are forced to stop drifting and to think what we are going to do. Either we avoid the situation or we tackle it. Whichever alternative is adopted, some 'thinking' has to be performed. Not all thinking is related to concrete, present situations, of course. The difficulty – although symbolically represented – may be remote from our present situation. Nevertheless it is something which is imposed upon us by circumstances largely beyond our control and we have to deal with the contingency somehow.

From this simple case the following points are clear:

(1) The term 'problem' applies to a very wide range of totally dissimilar situations. There are certain practical problems for engineers, and others for field-marshals; there are very different kinds of theoretical difficulty for mathematical physicists and systematic theologians. Young people in love and elderly people facing retirement may encounter problems, but of quite different kinds.

(2) Not all bits of logical thinking are solving or failing to solve problems. Going over an argument which one has considered and accepted previously, reading a piece of Latin verse that one has known since Sixth Form days (with occasional reaching for the dictionary), turning over the meanings of a concept which one has acquired in the past and used many times without ever having analysed it – all these activities are intelligent thinking activities, but none are quite 'problem' situations. Nor is asking a question and finding an answer always a case of having to meet and solve a problem.

Nevertheless, we frequently do have problems – of one kind or another – to deal with when we are thinking. It is therefore not surprising to find Professor Humphrey, of Oxford University, defining 'thought' at the end of his book as 'what happens in experience when an organism, human or animal, meets, recognizes, and solves a problem'. This definition is too narrow: but it does cover a wide range of different cases. Experimental psychologists can select specific problem-tasks for their subjects and observe the reactions which are displayed as each subject meets, recognizes, and attempts to solve his problem. The 'problem' can be defined clearly in behavioural terms, the variables can be known and controlled and the facts of problem-solving behaviour be elicited over a long series of investigations. Indeed, 'problem-solving' has become a minor field of investigation. It provides a good starting-point to any discussion on the psychology of thinking. Factors common to many thought processes are shown and 'leads' are suggested for further approaches to the investigation of thinking. Chapter Two will introduce the subject by describing studies of animals solving problems, and Chapter Three will discuss human problem-solving. From this discussion on problem-solving behaviour we will go on to discuss the formation and use of basic concepts in Chapters Four and Five. These four chapters will give some idea of what are the contents of typical thought processes: 'What a person does when he is thinking'.

We will then consider some of the conditions which determine the form and purpose of thinking activities. Learning, motivation, language, and the imaginative factors which make for creativity and originality will all be discussed. In the final chapter an attempt will be made to summarize the state of psychological knowledge in relation to human thinking and to elucidate further the aims and preoccupations of the psychologist in his attempt to gain knowledge.

One final point before we begin. We know very little about the psychology of thinking. What results are available are fragmentary and piecemeal. The psychologist cannot claim to be able to offer a complete description or a well-evidenced general theory to explain how we come to think in the way we do. This book gives an interim report on what psychologists have had to say on the subject so far. Work is going on which may radically alter the picture in ten or twenty years, when a much more thorough and integrated account of thinking will be available.

Furthermore, the psychologist would insist that his science will never be able to give more than a limited description of thinking. Other specialists can each contribute something to our understanding of thought from their own viewpoint. The physiologist may be able to tell us some day about the work of neural mechanisms in the brain and nervous system which guide and control thought; the cybernetician can show interesting analogies between the behaviour of living organisms who 'think' and that of electronic machines which simulate intelligent animal behaviour; the novelist and the poet can provide descriptions and images of how it feels when different human minds reflect in specific situations where the thoughts they have seem to have deep significance; the philosopher can bring out the subtle and often surprising implications of what we say when we talk about ourselves or other people as thinking – or when we express our thoughts in this terminology or in that; the logician shows according to what rules our statements must be related to each other if our thought is to avoid fallacy or absurdity and reach true or probable conclusions; and the psychiatrist can suggest how certain conflicts, phobias, repressions, or other emotional disturbances can distort our normal thinking.

The experimental psychologist lays no claim to be the only professional who thinks about thinking and communicates his conclusions on the nature of thought to others. He has the limited task of trying to apply scientific methods to the study of human and animal thinking and to discover the conditions which influence or determine characteristic thinking operations. The rest the psychologist leaves to other specialists. Especially – and with something like a sigh of relief – he leaves the task of synthesizing and evaluating the results of everybody's thinking about thought to the metaphysician.

So far as this book is concerned every reader must be his own metaphysician!

SELECTED REFERENCES

Bartlett, F. C. 'A Programme For Experiments on Thinking'. *Quarterly Journal of Experimental Psychology*, 1950.

What do we mean by 'Thinking'?

Bruner, J. S. 'Going Beyond the Evidence Given', in *Contemporary Approaches to Cognition* (Colorado Symposium). Cambridge, Mass. (Harvard University Press), 1957.

Humphrey, G. *Thinking*. London (Methuen), 1951.

Price, H. H. *Thinking and Experience*. London (Hutchinson), 1953.

Ryle, G. *The Concept of Mind*. London (Hutchinson), 1949.

Ryle, G. 'Thinking'. *Acta Psychologica*, 1953.

Ryle, G. *Proceedings of the Aristotelian Society*, 1951. (Supplementary Vol. xxv: 'Freedom, Language and Reality'.)

Vinacke, W. E. *The Psychology of Thinking*. New York and London (McGraw-Hill), 1952.

CHAPTER TWO

Problem-Solving Behaviour in Animals

THE starting-point for this inquiry into the psychology of thinking is the situation in which a problem may be said to exist for the agent. To recapitulate Humphrey's characterization of 'thought': 'Thinking ... may be provisionally defined as what occurs in experience when an organism, human or animal, meets, recognizes, and solves a problem.' This provisional definition was also favoured by Dewey, who pointed out that so long as our activity glides along smoothly, or as long as we allow our imagination to entertain fancies, there is no reflection. It is only when we are suddenly presented with a difficulty, obstruction, or frustration that we are forced to begin thinking. Thinking is part of our total response when we are presented with a problem which requires solution.

Many experiments have been designed and carried out to discover what happens, and under what antecedent conditions, when an organism meets a problem and attempts to solve it. Many of the most fascinating of these have been performed with animal subjects, chiefly rats, cats, and monkeys. It may be worth while to mention the reasons for using data derived from experiments with animals when investigating the conditions which govern thought processes.

In the first place, when using animal subjects it is possible to control most of the conditions under which the experiment takes place. The environment of the animal is simple compared with that of a human being.

It is sometimes possible to study and to regulate the entire life history of each animal subject, so that its previous training and learning can be known. Further, the behaviour of an animal can be thoroughly observed and described with some accuracy since what they do is relatively simple and little is missed if conditions of observation are good. Finally, we need not worry about the inner responses of the animal and can work within the conditions suggested by the early behaviourists as ideal for experimental psychology.

Of course, one must be careful in using the results in considering human behaviour. Human beings have a much more complicated nervous system than any other living creature and consequently have superior powers of observation and a more complex repertory of responses. What these animal studies do is merely to suggest broad analogies with human problem-solving. On the basis of such analogies hypotheses may be formed, which experiments with human subjects then proceed to test. There may be some analogies between human and animal behaviour. If there are not, at least there is a basis for comparison between the performances of different vertebrates when tackling problems.

EARLY EXPERIMENTS

One of the first psychologists to carry out such experiments was E. L. Thorndike, who was a professor at Columbia University, Ithaca, New York, and whose book *Animal Intelligence*, first published in 1911, still remains one of the classics of experimental psychology.

Thorndike developed two techniques for studying problem-solving behaviour in animals.

THE PUZZLE BOX

In this experiment a hungry cat is placed in a strong box one side of which is open, except that escape is prevented by bars through which the animal cannot squeeze. Through the bars the cat can see and sniff food. Escape can only take place if the captive animal operates a mechanism such as a lever or loop of string which opens a hatch at one side of the box. Usually there is only one such mechanism to be worked but the situation can be made more complicated by requiring the animal to operate two separate mechanisms successively before the hatch will open.

Thorndike carried out a simple experiment in which a particular cat was placed in the puzzle-box situation over and over again until it had learned how to escape by operating the lever or loop. The experiment was then repeated with a second animal and then with a third and so on.

It was discovered that the behaviour of each subject followed a similar pattern. At first the animal moved wildly about the box, pushing at the sides, clawing at the bars, and trying to squeeze through. At length, by accident, the mechanism was manipulated, the hatch opened, and the animal was able to escape and reach the food outside the box. As the experiment was repeated with each subject it was noticed that after a number of trials the frantic and useless attempts to claw and push out of the box were eliminated and the correct movement of operating the mechanism appeared earlier and earlier in the behaviour of the escape-oriented animal. In the end the animal could go over to the mechanism as soon as it was placed in the box and could operate it without hesitation or difficulty.

MAZE LEARNING

Thorndike also developed the maze as a piece of apparatus capable of many modifications and refinements. The animal is placed in a box. From this there is a single way of escape leading to a pathway bounded by walls and covered on top with a wire netting. In one of these mazes the route to be traversed is in the form of a square with two alternative pathways.

This is shown in a diagrammatic form in Figure 1. In order to get the food the hungry animal has to learn a sequence in running the maze. By using removable blocks different problems can be set the animal. For example it might have to go twice to the right followed by twice to the left. After a number of trials the correct habit emerges and remains dominant. The animal learns to eliminate errors. In a different type of maze there are simply a number of blind alleys between the start and the finish and the animal has to discover and retain the shortest route to the end.

How do animals manage to display such intelligent, adaptive behaviour? What they do, particularly in the puzzle-box situation, is very similar in some respects to human beings who have to solve a problem. At first there are a series of unsuccessful

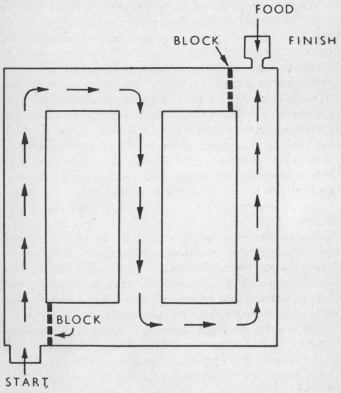

Figure 1

efforts to deal with the difficulty, these are dropped and replaced by exploratory behaviour, and finally the subject hits on an action leading to the solution of the problem. On repetition the action which initiates the solution is the one which is performed as soon as the subject finds himself facing the problem. This is called 'Trial and Error' learning.

The characteristics of such trial and error learning have been defined by R. S. Woodworth*:

(1) The organism must have a set towards a certain goal. (See Chapter Eight for a discussion of 'Set'.)

(2) There must be no obvious direct route to the goal.

(3) The situation must be explored in a more or less random fashion.

(4) By chance, 'leads' or 'clues' to the means of reaching the goal must emerge.

(5) Some of these leads must be tried out; those which work are retained and those which do not are dropped.

(6) A correct lead is found and the goal reached.

Thorndike developed a theory about intelligent behaviour on the assumption that trial and error learning is the basis of all learning. He suggested that the effect of a successful response is a condition of 'satisfaction' in the learner which ties that response to an appropriate stimulus in the problem situation. The stimulus, when next encountered in the problem situation, sets off the response with which it is associated and the response leads to a solution of the problem. Repetitions of this situation stamp in the stimulus-response sequence needed to solve the problem. Conversely, unsuccessful moves bring frustration and are stamped out of the repertory. There is no need to attribute to the animal any insight or symbolic representation of the situation. There is an automatic process for adapting needs to changes in the environment through the strengthening and weakening of stimulus-response bonds. The task of the psychologist is simply to explain the laws which govern the strengthening-weakening process and the emergence of correct responses within the problem situation. In Chapter Six this type of learning – 'instrumental conditioning' – will be described in detail.

For the present it is obvious that Thorndike's view applies well enough to the data of his own puzzle-box and maze experi-

* Woodworth, R. S. *Psychology*, Chapter 9. New York (Holt), 1940.

ments. However, there are reasons to suppose that more complex behaviour cannot be so readily explained in terms of Thorndike's theory. Indeed, there soon emerged a group of psychologists who were interested in problem-solving and who were critical of Thorndike's methods and theory.

In Germany, between the end of the First World War and the collapse of the Weimar Republic, a number of psychologists developed a new outlook to which the name Gestalt psychology was given. One of these, Wolfgang Köhler, maintained that the correct response required of the animal in the puzzle-box experiments of Thorndike is one which is abnormal for the animal to make. Cats do not escape from traps by manipulating levers; they push, claw, and scratch at obstacles and try to squeeze through openings or climb or jump to freedom. In fact they do all the things which Thorndike's set-up discourages. In Thorndike's experiments the correct move is bound to be reached by trial and error behaviour and stamped in by repetition simply because it is an unfamiliar sort of accomplishment for a cat to have to learn. The cat cannot perceive the mechanism which effects its escape, and even if it could it would not understand it. It is little wonder that the adaptive behaviour of the Thorndike experiment appears to be the product of conditioning. Nevertheless, it is possible that some animals can display something more akin to human insightful learning. The only way to find out whether they can or not is to conduct experiments which bring into play only such responses as come within the normal repertory of the animal.

Köhler used chimpanzees as his subjects, animals who display greater signs of intelligence than any others, and carried out a series of experiments the results of which are reported in his *The Mentality of Apes*.

KÖHLER'S EXPERIMENTS

In one experiment, a chimpanzee is placed in a cage and chained to a tree. A stick is placed within its reach. The animal handles the stick, gnaws at it, and eventually loses interest and drops it. After an interval a banana is placed outside the circle of which the chain forms the radius (therefore outside the animal's reach). After futile attempts to grasp the fruit with hands or feet, the chimpanzee seizes the stick, looks at the fruit, and then suddenly, clumsily, but quite deliberately, draws the fruit within reach. The stick has been used as an implement – a means-end relationship has somehow been grasped by the animal.

In another experiment, the chimpanzee is again caged. Outside the cage and beyond arm's-reach lie a bunch of bananas. Inside the cage and placed directly opposite the fruit is a short stick (A) (Figure 2) which is not long enough to reach the fruit. At the other end of the cage and outside the bars is a long stick (B).

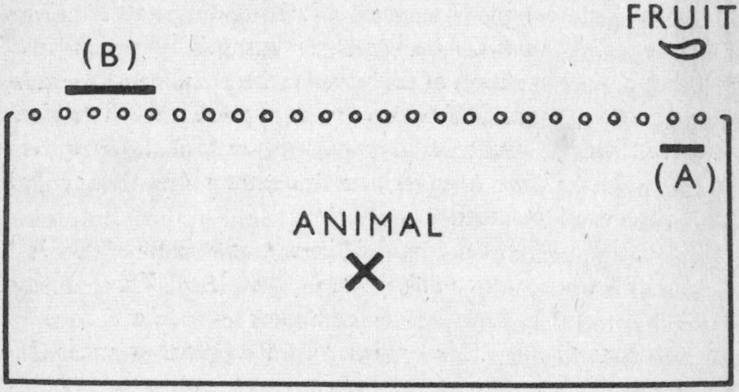

Figure 2

The problem set is quite a difficult one for the animal.

(1) The chimpanzee must take the short stick, go right to the farther end of the cage, and pull in the long stick.

(2) It must then return to the other end of the cage with the long stick and pull in the fruit.

The problem would seem to require a capacity for some kind of symbolic representation of the problem and the steps necessary for its solution. A plan is needed as a guide to activity.

The reactions of several animals to the situation were similar.

At first the short stick was used in an effort to pull in the fruit. Failure was followed by symptoms suggesting frustration and anger – the animal made a wild effort to tear down the strong bars. After a period of wandering round the cage, looking at the scene, the animal suddenly seized the short stick A, went over deliberately to the point opposite B and pulled in B with the aid of A, and ran excitedly to the point nearest the fruit – solving the problem by using the long stick.

Other experiments by Köhler required the animal to fit together two short sticks in order to make a long one for fruit-hauling or to pile boxes into a structure so as to reach fruit too high to reach by jumping.

Köhler claimed that the intelligent behaviour displayed by chimpanzees shows evidence of a capacity to 'think'. There is a grasp of relationships which are not immediately evident within a single perceptual field and so must be grasped by some kind of symbolic representation of the parts of the puzzle and the relations between them. Köhler argued further that the behaviour displays 'insight' and that 'insight' cuts out trial and error, the accidental stumbling on correct movements which are stamped in by successful repetitions.

Here then we meet our first difference among psychologists.

Animals can learn to solve simple problems. They exhibit what is reasonably described as intelligent behaviour in meeting and overcoming unfamiliar difficulties. How do they succeed in doing so? What means do they employ? Is it a matter of chance – the stamping in of the most suitable automatic response through external stimulation repeatedly 'setting off' the activity which pays? Or a more subtle kind of 'understanding' or 'insight' into the situation?

First, what does Köhler mean by 'insight'? The concept is by no means clear in meaning. There has been considerable misunderstanding owing to the ambiguity of the term. When we say of a human being that he has insight into a problem we mean that he knows what the situation is, what he intends doing, and how a solution can be achieved. This is not the meaning which

37

must necessarily be applied when the term is used of chimpanzee achievements. 'Insight' may equally well apply to the kind of solution which is achieved and the manner in which it is achieved: viz. the solution appears suddenly, complete, and controlled, without any symptom of 'trial and error' about it. To put it briefly, 'insight' is used in two senses:

(*a*) as a description of a pattern of behaviour observed in some problem-solving situations; (*b*) as a name of a postulated psychological process which controls behaviour.

The characteristics of insightful behaviour are easily listed. The successful response appears suddenly: and the response is easily repeated in future trials and is not easily forgotten or eliminated. This pattern contrasts with the other pattern in which errors are only gradually eliminated and the correct response only gradually acquired. There are, of course, many problem-solving situations which are neither 'insightful' nor instances of 'trial and error', but which lie half-way between the two extremes. Köhler's account, however, appears to be offering a somewhat special explanation. It is rather complicated and can only be made explicit if his conclusions about problem solving are stated in full.

There are at least four main conclusions which he emphasized:

(1) Organisms tend to approach the goal by the most direct path. Köhler believes that this response is 'determined without previous experience'. It is a species of instinct or innate drive.

(2) The changing pattern of the perceptual field is subject to tension whenever an obstruction or difficulty comes between the organism and the goal. This tension is a product of the frustration of goal-directed activity. The strength of the tension being determined: (*a*) by the particular desire for goal-state (e.g. a hungry animal has a powerful desire for food); (*b*) by the degree of attention directed towards the goal (e.g. if the goal stands out in a dominant manner in the usual field, attention is persistent and fixed on the goal).

(3) The behaviour of the organism in a problem-solving situa-

tion is the product of a field of forces set up by the unresolved tension within the organism's psychological (primarily perceptual) field, the pattern of this psychological field being determined by the goal influences mentioned in (2) and the physical factors in the external environment. If, for example, the animal turns its back on the goal object, tension slackens; or if a stick is placed within the animal's perceptual field and in a certain physical alignment to the goal-object, it becomes at once related to the total situation.

(4) These unstable, changing patterns of tension are suddenly reorganized by the perception of new routes leading directly to the goal. It is this sudden reorganization of the field which is 'insight'. What precisely is the nature of this psychological change is not explained by Köhler and his colleagues. It is something basic and irreducible. It is this feature of the Gestalt theory which leads its critics to accuse Köhler of introducing a mysterious agency to explain problem solving – such an appeal being a reversion to obsolete 'faculty psychology'.

There are, indeed, serious objections against the use of 'insight' as an explanatory concept. If we say that the subject suddenly gives the correct response to a problem *because* of a reorganization of his perceptual field, the explanation of this 'insight' is merely thrust back a stage further: we are still left with the question 'What made for this reorganization?; what factors (or "variables") may be singled out as determining the change?' This suddenness may be accidental and unconnected with any special 'understanding'. Spence discovered that chimpanzees, in a problem-solving experiment, sometimes adopted quite erroneous responses suddenly and kept on repeating them in spite of failure and frustration. Here suddenness and repetition were characteristics of error. Is there a perverse opposite of 'insight'?

CONTEMPORARY BEHAVIOURISM

What way out of this dispute can be found? More recent behaviouristic accounts suggest that trial and error learning is a much more subtle and complex process than the early behaviourists thought; further illustrations of animal problem-solving bring out the increasing subtlety of the theories evoked to explain what is observed to happen.

The basis of these more recent behaviouristic theories is to be found in a simple criticism directed against Köhler's experiments, namely that they fail to investigate the amount of previous training given to the successful animals. Using a young gorilla, Yerkes carried out similar investigations to those of Köhler. He points out that the animal only exhibits 'insightful behaviour' after very considerable preliminary training on simpler tasks. In some instances the experimenter had to demonstrate the correct movements in front of the gorilla so that it picked up the sequence by directly imitating its human instructor. Pechstein and Brown also conclude 'learning never takes place immediately when the problem is, in reality, new'.* Immediate solution – in experiments comparing the skill of gorillas, chimpanzees, and human children – can only occur if it is possible to transfer what has been previously learned. Thus the problem of explaining intelligent behaviour in the solving of problems depends upon our knowledge of how animals and human beings learn useful responses. It will be necessary to consider some of the conclusions which psychologists have tentatively reached on the subject of 'Learning' (especially in its relation to 'thinking') in Chapters Six and Seven.

For the present, let us consider one further crucial experiment. Most of Köhler's problem situations involved the putting together into an orderly sequence of several 'segments' of activity on the part of the animal subject. The chimpanzee has to move right away from the goal object (the fruit outside the bars of the cage). It has to pull off a branch of a bush, secure a long stick by using a short stick to pull it into the cage, or get hold of some other suitable instrument. Then it must return to its original position and finally carry out the 'fishing operation' of pulling in the fruit. What is it that binds these separate seg-

* *Journal of Educational Psychology*, 1939, 30.

ments of behaviour together into a 'rational' and ordered sequence?

N. R. F. Maier of Michigan University attempted to answer this question in a series of experiments on white rats, and the late C. L. Hull, one of the most distinguished of the psychologists of Yale University, has attempted to interpret the results of these experiments. The experimental design was simple. The animals were given training on segments of behaviour and then tested to see whether or not they would assemble these separate pieces of training into the one orderly sequence necessary for the solution of the problem.

Although Maier performed several different experiments, these had a common plan. The situation summarized here is taken from C. L. Hull's conventionalized form of Maier's 'Reasoning in Rats' situations.*

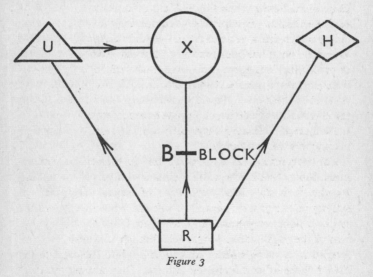

Figure 3

The four goal-boxes, U, X, H, and R (Figure 3), are set on

* See G. E. Osgood's admirable study, *Method and Theory in Experimental Psychology*, Chapter 14.

tables and connected by identical raised runways. Each box is constructed so as to make it as distinctive from the rest as possible – having a specific shape and floor covering (rats have sensitive foot-pads); e.g. X might have flossy, silk flooring, U cold metal with rough furrows, H warm, polished metal, and R layers of rubber.

While training on one pathway (e.g. R to U) all other pathways were blocked so that the animal could easily learn the sequence.

The sequence of training events was as follows: (*a*) from R to X for a food reward; (*b*) from U to X for a food reward; (*c*) from R to U for a water drink reward; (*d*) from R to H for a water drink reward.

Care was taken to make each segmental habit firmly established and equal to each other segmental habit.

Having been thoroughly trained in each of these four habits each animal was then put through the following test:

The animal is placed hungry at R with the direct and previously learned pathway R – X blocked at B. This left R – U and R – H open. The problem is to discover whether the rat will run towards U and thence round to X (a roundabout route to X, where a food reward waits, requiring the putting together of two behaviour segments, R – U, U – X) more often than towards H (previously learned route to a drink reward).

The result of the experiments was clear-cut. The rats do this – they appear to choose the more complicated road R – U – X instead of R – H. But why? How do they manage it? Maier did not hesitate to attribute *some* kind of reasoning to his rats. While it remains at R the rat must somehow represent the completed path to X via U (and perhaps contrast it with the path R – H). The rat cannot talk to itself, but some implicit, covert, inner symbolic process must be at work to guide the rat in its successful solution of the problem.

C. L. Hull, however, regarded the attribution of some reasoning process to the rat as unnecessary. He wanted to be able to explain its behaviour solely in terms of a series of stimulus-response situations. His view requires a demonstration that the stimulus pattern at R is more strongly associated with the total response of running towards U than with the response of running towards H at the time at which the test is made. Hull gives this explanation in terms of his own extremely complex theory of learning-behaviour (made more difficult owing to his liking for the use of formulae derived from mathematical logic). It is, however, possible to give some indication of Hull's view without resorting to his terminology. Hull argues as follows:

(1) The hungry rat runs, during training, from U to X. In time, parts of the total goal-reaction (getting and eating food) become conditioned to stimuli received at U, become, so to speak, short-circuited, and occur while the animal is in the box U. That is, there is an association between the feels of box U and the feels of box X such that the former arouses anticipatory responses toward the latter. This leads to a further conditioning, running from U to X whenever the anticipatory X-feels arise.

(2) When subsequently running from R to U for a drink when thirsty, the stimuli at U elicit anticipatory food-taking reactions as a learned habit: the animal although not hungry has these reactions reinforced through the 'satisfaction' of drinking. R – U becomes a rewarding run, as well as U – X, the link being arrival at U. By a similar short-circuiting, being at R comes to have a link with the rewards at U, and via U with rewards at X.

(3) On the test run, the rat is hungry at R. R – X is blocked. The reactions at R are anticipatory food-taking reactions. These are conditioned to running to U for water rather than to running to H for water, and this tips the balance in favour of the R – U response. This response is more strongly reinforced than the R – H response. Once the animal reaches U, the problem is solved, since it has already a conditioned response to run U – X for food rewards.

Hull predicted that once the rat gets to U from R, the anticipatory responses that are set off there by the U stimuli, together with the short-circuited X anticipations (conditioned to U stimuli), will make the rat increase its speed of running on the final stretch from U to X. This, in fact, was what happened – the successful prediction giving some slight confirmation to the theory.

This complicated deduction depends on the establishment of a mediating response to bridge the two segments of learned responses; that is, the anticipatory food-taking reactions must be associated with box U when the animals run there from R for water when they are thirsty.

If training followed a different order; if, for example, the water runs (from R to U and from R to H) were established before the training on U to X for food, Hull would predict purely random or chance choices on the final test trials. This would be the case because there would be no way for the food-taking reactions and their stimuli to become associated with running towards U.

As Osgood points out,* if this different training sequence were actually followed in an experiment, with all the variables adequately controlled, and if the rats did better than chance (that is, in terms of the mathematical theory of chance) then this result would be good evidence for suggesting that rats can reason. This experiment does not appear to have been carried out at the time of writing.

This behaviouristic explanation of insightful problem-solving is given in terms of a particular theory of learning and would not be acceptable to all psychologists. In common with many such theories it postulates processes which cannot be observed nor which can be inferred with certainty from any observable factors. Such postulated processes serve the function of mediators or links between the known stimulus situation and the observed pattern of responses. Such, for example, are Hull's 'anticipatory food-taking responses', which are a detached fragment of food-finding and food-eating behaviour and which become conditioned to cues at the start of a maze. How do we know that such responses are occurring? They cannot be observed nor can they be immediately deduced from anything which a rat does in the box. Nor can we determine when a

* Osgood, *Method and Theory of Experimental Psychology*.

shift has taken place in a hierarchy of established habits. The Gestalt view which postulates changes in the reorganization of the perceptual field of a chimpanzee is equally speculative. Of course, it is hoped that some day our knowledge of the functioning of the brain and nervous system of the subjects will enable the psychologist to account for intelligent behaviour in neurological terms. That day seems remote, however, and we have to accept the speculative nature of psychological explanations for the time being. This makes it difficult to decide between one theoretical model and another and makes differences of opinion inevitable when it comes to interpreting the experimental facts.

It is not our immediate purpose to enter into these controversies and to decide in favour of one school or the other. What we want to know are the general facts about animal intelligence as a basis for comparison with human performances.

From what has been said certain broad conclusions emerge. Firstly, it is certain that many animals exhibit intelligent behaviour of an elementary kind in tackling and solving problems; this is especially the case with chimpanzees. Some of these problems cannot be solved by rigidly formed habits. Thus the beginnings of intelligence can be detected lower down the evolutionary scale.

Secondly, experiments with animals make it clear that adaptive behaviour is largely explicable from a knowledge of the past experience of the animal. Intelligent behaviour is either learning something new or the adaptation of former learning to a slightly unfamiliar problem. Also most animals have to be given some incentive to solve a problem. They have to be kept hungry and given food as a sort of reward for solving the problem or else they have to be placed in a noxious situation from which it is probable that they will strive to escape. There must be a drive or need active in order that the problem shall be 'recognized'. It may be that learning and motivation, at a much more complex developmental level, are crucial in human problem solving as well.

Finally, there are characteristic patterns of behaviour which are repeated by different animals in different situations – trial and error and sudden insight, for example. These in a more sophisticated form may occur with human subjects.

It is, of course, a far cry from the intelligent problem-solving behaviour of Köhler's chimpanzees to the human child learning to talk and the older child learning to reason logically. There remains a gap between animal intelligence and human thought which is considerable. Nevertheless human thought may have its origins in similar *kinds* of operations to those practised in a simpler way by animals. And some basic types of human skill may have their parallel lower down the scale of life. The study of animals, like the study of children or primitive peoples, may give us clues regarding what is crucial and important in the make-up of the civilized adult.

SELECTED REFERENCES

Hull, C. L. 'The Mechanism of the Assembly of Behaviour Segments in Novel Combinations Suitable for Problem Solution'. *Psychological Review*, 1935.

Köhler, W. *The Mentality of Apes*. London (Routledge & Kegan Paul), 1925. Pelican Books, 1957.

Maier, N. R. F. 'Reasoning in White Rats'. *Comparative Psychology Monographs*, 1929.

Osgood, C. E. *Method and Theory in Experimental Psychology*, Part IV. Oxford, 1953.

Thorndike, E. L. *Animal Intelligence*. London (Macmillan), 1911.

CHAPTER THREE

Problem-Solving Behaviour in Human Beings

PROBLEM-solving experiments on human subjects are usually less straightforward than those performed with animals. With human subjects the variables are difficult to determine and isolate, and it is rarely possible to devise methods of measurement. The most effective method is to present a problem to a subject and get him to think out loud during his efforts to solve it. The subject is closely observed by the experimenter and his responses are noted down. Afterwards the subject is asked to think back over his attempt and to tell what was happening, how he hit upon a particular approach, what changes occurred in his thoughts during the critical phases of the solution. Many different situations are used – problems in plane geometry, anagrams, word-association tests, the manual disentangling of metal puzzles ('twisted serpents', 'interlocked nails') and technical difficulties in medicine, or business administration problems.

It might be asked at this point: 'Why doesn't an examination of logic help us to discover the methods we use when we think out problems?' The answer, to put it simply, is that logic helps us to deal with the products of thinking but does not study the processes which go on when we are described as thinking. Logic provides us with precise criteria whereby the truth or falsity of conclusions may be tested or the consistency or inconsistency of reasoned argument be assessed. Logic gives us hypothetical truths – it shows that if the statements p and q are taken as true, then certain conclusions *must* follow: but logic does not enable us to establish the truth of our ultimate premises, nor does it enable us to interpret their precise meaning in specific context, or even to decide whether or not p is meaningful or absurd. Nor can formal logic help us to search for, select, and interpret the data required for the solution of any concrete problem – it merely supplies forms and rules which enable us to organize and analyse such data. If we want to study what happens when a person thinks out a problem, we must either conduct psychological experiments or use other empirical means for collecting and examining facts – requiring subjects to answer a questionnaire, or culling the papers of scientific workers for hints regarding how they think.

One of the earliest investigations into typical problem-solving behaviour was that of the American psychologist Ruger, who published his findings in *Archives of Psychology* (N.Y.) in 1910. He studied the relation between motor activity and verbalization by giving his subjects mechanical puzzles, familiar in the stock of any toyshop (twisted serpents, interlaced circles, the ball wedged in the star): each puzzle required the subject to manipulate the metal until the separate pieces were disentangled.

Ruger noted several common reactions:

(1) Most subjects attempt to pin down the crucial area ('It must slip through this space') and the right temporal order ('But first I must get it loosened here').

(2) Many subjects suddenly find the puzzle has come out without having done anything deliberately to produce the solution. They then analyse the situation retrospectively. ('How did I do it? I had the two pieces like this, then ...')

(3) If the crucial principle is discovered, the subject usually traces the details of each separate step or move. But the general principle comes first.

DUNCKER'S INVESTIGATION

Much more complicated problems have been set by K. Duncker, a German psychologist who was a pupil of Wertheimer, the founder of Gestalt psychology. He confined his investigation to problems requiring abstract reasoning. His interesting experiments were designed, not so much to test specific hypotheses, as to evoke general facts about reasoning. They were meant to open up the field and supply data for further investigation rather than to answer questions or confirm theories. Again, as in Ruger's experiment, the subject had to talk out loud during his problem-solving.

Here is one of his crucial experiments. The problem given for solution was a practical one.

'If a human being has a stomach tumour and surgical operation proves impracticable, how can the tumour be destroyed by ray treatment: the difficulty is that the rays destroy healthy tissue as well as diseased tissue and the tumour is completely surrounded by healthy tissue.'

One subject, taking half an hour to reach his final solution, tried out the following lines of thought:

(1) Send the rays through the oesophagus (the gullet).

(2) By giving chemical injections, render the healthy tissue insensitive to the rays.

(3) Expose the tumour by bringing it towards the surface of the body.

All these suggestions are impracticable: the subject was given reasons for ruling them out.

(4) A new line was then tried. Is it possible to decrease the intensity of the rays so that they do not destroy healthy tissue and yet destroy the tumour? The intensity of the rays ought to be rendered variable. But how? Several false leads were tried ('Swallow something to protect stomach linings': 'Adapt healthy tissue to rays by weak application which gets stronger'); and finally:

(5) Somehow divert or diffuse the rays. Suddenly the solution came: 'Send a broad and weak bundle of rays through a lens in such a way that the tumour lies at the focal point and thus receives intensive radiation'. This is the sort of solution required by the problem. The most efficient solution is to cross several weak bundles of rays at the tumour so that the intensity which destroys tissue is achieved *only* at that part.

Duncker gave his subjects several different types of problem – anagrams, mathematical problems, mechanical puzzles. From a number of diverse experiments he drew general conclusions regarding the 'searching for solution' phase of inquiry.

How do people actually work towards a solution, according to Duncker?

(1) The mistaken solutions put forward are not inappropriate. The subject seems to keep the basic relations between tumour, healthy tissues, and rays before him and makes suggestions which fit at least some of the facts. It is impracticable to pass rays down the oesophagus, but the idea of getting rays through an opening without their touching healthy tissues is the sound suggestion behind this incorrect solution.

(2) Each proposal is a re-formulation of the problem. The basis of a new hypothesis is the flexible shifting of all the factors which make up the problem situation in relation to each other. This 'shifting' is the defining character of abstract reasoning.

(3) Any hypothesis is judged on its functional characteristics. A number of alternatives may have an equivalent functional value: (e.g. either 'Get the tumour moved somehow so that it can be exposed to the rays or removed surgically without other tissues being involved', or 'Get the rays focused on the tumour but avoiding the surrounding tissue'). Once hypotheses which are functionally sound are put forward, practical considerations determine which is the useful one to implement.

(4) Blind solutions are restricted to the specific problem-situation in which they occur. In situations in which the functional characteristics are grasped, the solution can be transferred and applied in a variety of situations.

In strictly rational problem-solving, then, the subject analyses the situation in order to discover the materials involved and the crucial relations whose reorganization results in the solution becoming clear. The goal must be analysed, too, in order that the subject can see what must be done in order to move from the 'recognition of the problem' state to the 'final solution' state. However, strictly rational problem-solving is rare.

Most solutions are achieved through what Duncker calls 're-sonance'. 'Resonance' is the largely automatic application of previous experience to the present situation – by means of cogni-tive-perceptual responses. These cognitive-perceptual responses are set off through reactions to 'signals' from the immediate environment in which the problem is set. Various possibilities are suggested by what the subject perceives in the present and by his reactions to present stimuli as determined by past experience. Success comes through, more or less, chance re-formulations and changes in the presented data – the solution emerging from a particular reorganization of the 'psychological field'. Sometimes the solution appears suddenly, sometimes there has to be a search for the source of the difficulty and the working out of a practical means-end relationship: problem-solving can exhibit either trial and error or a partially analytical approach when 'resonance effects' determine the solution.

WERTHEIMER'S VIEWS

Duncker acknowledged his debt to his former teacher, Max Wertheimer. Wertheimer worked with Köhler at Berlin University in the 1920s. Although Wertheimer's work was only published, posthumously, in 1945, it contained the results of investigations going back to the early years of the century from which Duncker and many others benefited as pupils of Wertheimer.

Wertheimer carried out a series of informal experiments with school-children. In one of these he showed the children, using conventional text-book methods, how to find the area of any rectangle. He illustrated his demonstration by showing that, if the height of a rectangle is conceived as so many little squares, then the area will be equal to the total number of vertical columns of little squares: the principle, $a \times b$, can then be illustrated as 'seeing how many columns of squares of a given height are included in the rectangle'. Wertheimer claimed that this approach achieved insight into the operation – it exhibits its structure, showing the relation between the different dimensions of the rectangle and the relation of parts fitting into a whole. The one consistent 'idea' behind this method of instruction helps the children to think in a developing, unfolding style from beginning to end. Once this was achieved, Wertheimer set the children a problem: 'Find the area of any parallelogram'.

A child of 5 asked for scissors. Making a vertical cut which divided the parallelogram into two parts (ADE and DCBE – see Figure 4), she moved section ADE from the left to the right of the figure. The rectangle thus formed was obviously equal in area to the parallelogram. The area of the rectangle could be determined by the method which the child had been taught. The child had realized that if only the parallelogram could be transformed into a rectangle of equal area the familiar method for determining areas could be applied. The solution rose from the perception that ADE=BCF. Insight and perception of relationships aided the child to achieve a solution.

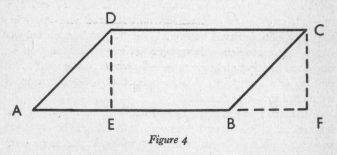

Figure 4

Wertheimer – from a whole series of problem-solving tests of which the above is only one specimen – arrived at a general theory about problem-solving.

Problem-solving, for Wertheimer, depends on a grasping of the structural and functional relationships of the problem situation. The 'inner relations' of the situation must be discovered and each particular situation has its *own* distinctive set of requirements: finding these and reorganizing the situation in the light of this discovery is the key to solution. Problem-solving is not the automatic application of established habits or behaviour patterns to stereotyped situations, nor is it the application of definable principles. It is a *dynamic* process growing out of, and shaped by, each specific situation.

'Such a process is not just the sum of several steps, not an aggregate of several operations, but the growth of one line of thinking out of the gaps in the situation.'*

One feature of problem-solving which is important for Wertheimer is the 'recentring' of the perceptual field which opens the way to the solution. There are 'structural' stresses and strains which have to be resolved by the forming or grasping of a new pattern of relationships. Each problem limits the range of such patterns which must 'fit' the goal-state, and solution is simply the recognition of a practical reorganization. The achievement of this reorganization is brought about by varying the mode of attack, changing the basic concept in terms of which the situation is described and interpreted, and shifting the principles upon which hypotheses or 'leads' are framed. The tensions set up by the problem are only relieved when the solution is actually achieved – these tensions help to keep the subject active. Thus problem-solving is an activity which can only be described inadequately in terms of abstract features. It is a striving and struggling with a configuration the structure of which changes with the effort.

Wertheimer concludes his definition by emphasizing the importance of past experience on present capacity to deal with concrete problems – aiding insightful adaptations in some cases and preventing intelligent behaviour in others by strengthening blind, piecemeal attacks.

THE GENERAL CHARACTERISTICS OF PROBLEM-SOLVING

It may be concluded that there are clearly distinguishable phases in a typical cycle of problem-solving behaviour.

(1) The subject must recognize and fixate the problem. In

* Wertheimer, M. *Productive Thinking*. New York (Harper), 1945, p. 50.

human problem-solving it is rarely the case that random movements are set off by a blind undirected feeling of frustration. There is a difficulty, obstruction, or frustration which has to be pinned down and made capable of description and analysis. The problem, once known for what it is, may be met by activity or avoided by flight or withdrawal – but it is not a problem at all until it is *defined*.

(2) Search or exploration of the field within which the problem exists is the next step after identification. This stage may be marked by passive observation of the data, careful inspection of the materials involved, or the interrelations which have to be traced and reorganized, or it may involve reflection on possible hypotheses suggested through an examination of perceptual data. Sometimes manipulation of materials, or trial and error moves take place during exploration: sometimes much verbalization, 'working it out in one's head', characterizes this phase.

(3) Analysis of the problem follows. The results of identification and exploration must be sorted out and, if possible, a plan constructed which reorganizes the situation so that there is a continuous series of stages between confrontation with the problem and final solution. If this is not possible, or if it doesn't work out, the problem must be restated and leads suggested for testing.

(4) Finally comes attack, involving the tackling of preliminary parts before the final stages can be accomplished: such partial solution, by getting sub-problems solved, may be necessary at first. Associated with this and earlier phases are emotional reactions – anxiety or tension, disappointment, anger, satisfaction, relief, according to progress or failure! Such emotional factors may have considerable effects on the course of the problem-solving attempt and may influence the final issue.

In many simple problems these four phases may become telescoped in a single, swift coordinated phase of activity – but in complex situations all phases may be distinctly observed.

Although these are the most general characteristics of human problem-solving it is obvious that many individual differences appear; these are especially evident in the method of attack employed. Durkin has attempted to classify these differences and he is careful to insist that his distinctions are not to be taken as indicating rigidly exclusive types: the mode of attack is often changed within the course of a particular problem, and there are transitional and mixed styles. One variety is that of 'insightful behaviour' already discussed. A second variety is 'trial and error' with retrospective understanding of how the problem came to be solved: a third is 'analytical approach' – here the emphasis is on gradual, step-by-step efforts: a mixture of insight, trial and error, and logical thinking. This latter variety lacks 'the groping, indefinite, accidental-solution' pattern of trial and error and the sudden intuitive reorganization of the whole problem characteristic of insight. It conforms more to logical argument as set down in writing – yet without its rigour.

CONTROLLING CONDITIONS

So far, only descriptions of problem-solving situations have been presented together with their abstracted general characteristics. Fact-finding experiments, which give the investigator a systematic mode of attack based on favourable conditions of observation, have yielded a general picture of what human beings do and their manner of doing it when problem-solving.

It is important to discover what conditions govern such behaviour – what are the variables without which such behaviour could not occur at all and the particular concurrence of which makes such behaviour the particular phenomenon that it is observed to be. We can consider the conditions which emerge from experimental investigations to be the most prominent.

EXPERIENCE

Perhaps the most important line of research is the role of past learning on present performance. How exactly experience influences behaviour is a question which takes us to the very core of psychology and, indeed, into many investigations far beyond the scope of the present chapter. (See Chapters Six and Seven:

learning, transfer, set.) However, some conclusions must be mentioned here. For example, two experiments by N. R. F. Maier show the importance of 'direction' or 'set' in problem-solving.

Maier's experiments on human beings owe something to his study of the integration of separate behaviour segments in rats which was described in Chapter Two (p. 41). Given practice on separate parts of a problem solution can human subjects integrate these segments into a serial activity without being given

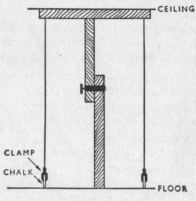

Figure 5

some 'direction' or 'set' – a clue to the manner in which the integration takes place? The answer of the experiment seems to be that human subjects are helpless without such a guide or integrating control. Past experience and present perception come together only through the operation of this factor. The task in the experiment was simply to construct two pendulums, each of which had to swing over a marked point on the floor. The subjects were supplied with a limited set of materials – two kinds of clamp, chalk, wire, and three lengths of wood. The solution was relatively easy. (See Figure 5.)

(1) The chalk had to be fixed in a clamp and the clamp tied to

a length of wire which could be suspended from the ceiling to the floor.

(2) Next a pole had to be constructed which reached from the floor to the ceiling by clamping two separate lengths of wood together.

(3) Finally the third piece of wood had to act as a wedge between the ceiling and the upright pole constructed in stage 2.

Then the two pendulums could hang from either extremity of the wedged wood – as shown in the sketch.

The direction, when it was given, was a statement uttered by the experimenter to the effect that it would be easy to solve the problem if one could only hang the pendulums from two points on the ceiling.

The problem was given to the following groups:

(1) Control Group. The problem was given without any preliminaries.

(2) Part solutions were shown to the second group (e.g. chalk clamped as in the sketch), but no attempt was made to relate these to the problem as a whole.

(3) Part solutions were shown to the third group and related to the problem in various ways (i.e. it was pointed out that one part solution was the first step to make in solving the problem and was related in such and such a way to the second).

(4) The problem was presented and the direction was given but nothing more.

(5) Part solutions as to group 3 plus the direction.

Several different types of solution were attempted – tripods were constructed with the three pieces of wood, but only one group, No. 5, gained any successful or correct solutions. Eight out of twenty-two subjects in this group solved the problem, whereas only one out of sixty-two subjects in the first three groups was successful. Moreover, a higher number of the failures in Group 5 were on the right lines. Direction – added to hints about part solutions – made for a considerable difference.

A second experiment of Maier's added a further control.

The problem was to construct a hat-rack given two wooden

spars and a clamp. Three groups were given the task.

(1) The first had previously helped the experimenter to construct a piece of laboratory apparatus which included a similar structure to the finished hat-rack. Specimens of this apparatus were deliberately placed in the room for the hat-rack problem – a visual clue for those who could recognize it.

(2) The second group had helped to construct the apparatus, but no specimens were left in the room for the hat-rack puzzle. They had to rely on memory and associations.

(3) The third group had no previous experience in construction apparatus.

The successful solution was relatively easy (see Figure 6).

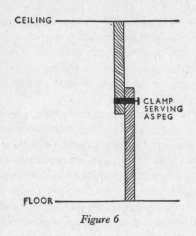

Figure 6

72 per cent of group 1, 48 per cent of group 2, and 24 per cent of group 3 were successful.

How is it that one group is much better than the others in solving the problem? Presumably previous constructions with similar materials help in drawing the subjects' attention to the crucial 'reorganization' factor, namely 'use the clamp as a peg for hanging the hats on at the same time as it helps to make two short pieces of wood into a pole which wedges between floor and ceiling'. The 'set' or 'direction' comes from previous experience in the making of apparatus which included the 'hat-rack' solution. In a similar way the presence of scissors helped the child to solve Wertheimer's parallelogram problem. There are evidently 'mediation processes' at work which assist problem-solving and render it more efficient. These processes are relevant to most forms of intelligent behaviour and are the key to our understanding of the role 'experience' plays in thinking successfully.

The behaviourists tend to regard such meditation processes as a function of previous training: the Gestalt school regard them as part of the spontaneous reorganization of the perceptual-cognitive field (which is 'insight'). Both theories probably contain part of the truth of the matter. But from whatever source they spring – perceptual cues, symbolic recall, conditioning, instructions – appropriate 'set' or 'direction' greatly facilitates problem-solving.

MOTIVES

It is also known that human thinking is determined by motivational factors. If the subject is over-involved emotionally in a problem, he is less likely to be successful than if he is moderately motivated. Over-anxiety, intense dislike of the situation, annoyance or anger, clearly upset the balance and concentration of the subject. On the other hand, indifference, half-heartedness, over-confidence, are equally disturbing: persistence and application can only come from a certain degree of interest and concern. A moderate but effective motivation is needed: How are we motivated in meeting and solving problems? What factors determine our attitudes and interests? These are questions which we must deal with later.

CONCEPTS

The concepts in terms of which the problem situation is described and interpreted have a considerable effect on success or failure. When concepts are discussed in Chapters Four and Five it will be clear that some concepts help, and others hinder, practical thinking.

It is often helpful – as Wertheimer and Duncker suggested – to verbalize freely when examining the problem situation (we often do talk to ourselves when puzzling something out) – changing one's terms, analysing the meaning of what one says when abstract notions are involved in interpreting the problem. Only by shifting the meanings can the fixated concept (which is blocking insight) become weakened and removed. We have to get rid of the wrong ideas, and such ideas are only too easy to come by. This is another topic for later elucidation.

EXPLORATION

Shifting, not only one's 'ideas about the situation', but also one's physical position in relation to the problem may affect efficiency. If it is a practical problem, the field can be explored and materials can be manipulated in 'trial and error' preliminary trials. If the problem cannot be dealt with in physical activity, one can always imagine possible alternatives – as in the stomach tumour problem of Duncker's. Alternative hypotheses can be worked out before being actually put to test.

FURTHER CONDITIONS INFLUENCING THINKING

There are many other factors which seem relevant to problem-solving but which have not yet been adequately investigated by psychologists.

It is obvious, for example, that very young people and very old people are less adept at dealing with a large range of problems than mature adults in the prime of life. What is the relation between age and problem-solving capacities? Are some age-groups better all round than any others, or do certain age-groups show aptitudes for some types of problem rather than others? Do capacities change in any consistent manner as the subject grows older or are capacities distributed over the age-scale in an irregular manner? Is age a relevant factor at all? These questions seem important, but unfortunately cannot be answered clearly at present.

Again, it is accepted that individuals differ considerably in their general intelligence. Differences in I.Q. probably correlate with specific differences in problem-solving behaviour. But how precisely do differences in intelligence relate to differences in thinking performances of the kind studied in problem-solving?

Finally, it might be worth while to study the pathology of thought processes in psychotic and neurotic case-histories and to compare the modes of attack, patterns of behaviour, etc., of mental patients with those of normal people. Clinical data can often be illuminating in studying the so-called normal cases. One of the limitations of psychological studies of problem-solving is that these are based on laboratory data: the subject is presented with a stimulus situation and his reactions are studied under experimental conditions. Case-histories give us actual thinking in typical situations – even when these are abnormal – and it may be that the processes which mediate between the presentation of a problem and its solution may be best studied on a comparative basis: namely, 'How do normal people differ from pathological cases in thinking out problems of various kinds?'

The conditions which determine problem-solving behaviour in human subjects are complex in the extreme. Experiments in the laboratory, observations in the classroom and clinic, do no more than suggest some of the basic responses involved and the most obvious conditions which determine these responses. So far, what has emerged is a general sketch, the details of which have to be completed by future psychological research. It may be some time before a thorough knowledge of the elementary basis of behaviour is possible (learning theory is still in a comparatively early stage of development). And even if the basic processes were thoroughly understood, the task of relating problem-solving behaviour to other major psychological functions (e.g. perception, creative imagination, the 'unconscious' factors of psycho-pathological interest) would present great difficulties. The formulation of reliable and testable laws of behaviour in any field seems a long way in the future.

Nevertheless much progress has been made when one considers the state of psychological knowledge a hundred, or even fifty, years ago. The fields of investigation are beginning to be more clearly defined, specific problems are coming forward, and methods of dealing with them are becoming increasingly scientific. One field, in particular, is important: the controversial topic of the operations which constitute human and animal learning and the conditions under which these processes function has received considerable attention. When a new problem is tackled or a concept formed in order to interpret perceptual data, the past experience of the organism is applied and organized in some way. All thinking depends upon learning. In order to clarify the present state of our knowledge of thinking it is necessary to say something about the psychology of learning.

Before discussing learning, one of the most essential conditions of thought, it is necessary to review another field of inquiry into the actual content of thinking: namely, the formation, retention, and use of basic concepts in terms of which experience is interpreted. Chapters Four and Five will be devoted to the study of concepts and we will go on to 'learning' in Chapter Six.

SELECTED REFERENCES*

Duncker, K. 'A Qualitative (Experimental and Theoretical) Study of Productive Thinking (Solving of Comprehensible Problems)'. *Journal of Genetic Psychology*, 1926, 33, 642–708.

Duncker, K. *On Problem Solving* (transl. Lynnes Lees). Psychological Monographs, 1945, No. 270.

Osgood, C. E. *Method and Theory in Experimental Psychology*. Chapter 14. Oxford, 1953.

Vinacke, W. E. *The Psychology of Thinking*. Chapter 9. New York and London (McGraw-Hill), 1952.

Wertheimer, M. *Productive Thinking*. New York (Harper), 1945.

* See also p. 216.

CHAPTER FOUR

Concepts and their Attainment

IN human thinking the use of concepts is one essential factor. For one thing, as A. H. Maslow has pointed out, when we perceive a familiar object or event we rarely attend to its idiosyncratic characteristics. If we did we would spend a considerable time allowing our senses to play over the stimulus factors, 'soaking' our attention in the unique properties of the particular perception. Instead we quickly catalogue what we perceive in a matter of seconds – using a ready-made set of concepts. For example, we glance at the dining-room table and recognize a new bowl of fresh flowers. The concept 'flower' indicates both the configuration that we are seeing, smelling, and touching, and also relates this present impression to an indefinite class of similar ones in the past. Thus to identify what we perceive as 'flowers' is partly being able to use a particular word. But it is primarily the making of a consistent response to a particular group of stimuli. Even if we had no words we could still learn to respond differently to a bowl of flowers and to a rattlesnake. Children learn to discriminate and recognize certain persons and things some time before they learn to speak: they have a small and imperfectly formed set of concrete concepts in terms of which they respond consistently to familiar objects.

The basis of a concept is a response (or perhaps a readiness to respond in certain ways rather than others). This response is of a particular kind when it serves as the basis of a concept.

Firstly, there must be some degree of 'generality of application'. If a person is confronted with a strange object he may react by saying 'Well it looks like some unusual vegetable or fruit'. In saying this he generalizes from what is familiar in order to categorize the new and unidentified object. The stranger is placed in some familiar category and treated accordingly.

Secondly, there must be some differentiation among the cases to which the concept applies. Tomatoes, lettuces, carrots, and kidney-beans are all 'vegetables' and yet have markedly different properties of colour, smell, taste, shape, etc. Instances of a concept need not be exactly similar to each other in every respect.

Finally, the same set of objects and events are not necessarily tied to one particular concept. By shifting the concept one can place a particular item in a totally different class. For instance, if we have a number of wooden blocks of different shapes, sizes, and colours we can sort these into a number of different classes: all the red pieces or all blues, all greens and all yellows can form separate groups whose defining attribute is 'colour'; or all square blocks, all triangular, all rectangular can be placed in separate 'shape' categories; or all tall blocks separated from all squat ones. Each category is based on a consistent response towards each of its instances – yet any item can change its category according to the concept being used.

So far the sort of concept we have been examining is based on the familiar trick of classifying or categorizing. There are many varieties of concept, but the class concept is the type which has been selected for scrutiny by experimental psychologists. It may be that this, almost exclusive, attention paid to classification as an exemplification of conceptualizing derives from Aristotle's logic (which is based upon relations of class inclusion and exclusion) and from the fact that few people are aware of the revolutionary changes in logic in the present century. But this is not to deny that classification is a useful device in enabling us to interpret our experience.

Professor J. S. Bruner, whose experiments are to be described later in this chapter, has pointed out some of the advantages ensuing from the use of class concepts. For one thing, classification reduces the complexity of our environment and thus makes it easier to deal with. There are seven million colour differences to which human beings can respond, but we use only a limited number of colour concepts in discriminating objects and in describing their sensory properties. Again, we are enabled to identify objects and events by placing them quickly into preconceived categories; this reduces the strain on our nervous system by rendering recognition or identification automatic and by reducing the amount of learning we have to tackle. If we did not categorize or classify automatically we would be faced with the exhausting and complicated task of relating every particular item in our experience to every other item in the context of their occurrence. We would flounder in the immediate concrete situation and be unable to interpret it. Indeed this is what happens to certain patients suffering from disease or damage to the brain. If, for example, such patients are asked to pick up a comb from a table and bring it to the physician, what the patient does is to pick up the comb and begin combing his hair. Such patients cannot even place little bits of coloured wool in red groups, green groups, etc. – they have lost their capacity to classify. Finally, classification is an immediate guide to appropriate adaptive behaviour. Once an object is classified not as an edible mushroom but as a poisonous fungus, we desist from eating it and prevent others from tasting it.

DEFINITION OF THE TERM 'CONCEPT'

Professor W. E. Vinacke of Hawaii University in his book *The Psychology of Thinking* summarizes what the term 'concept' means in psychology.

A concept is basically a system of learned responses the purpose of which is to organize and interpret the data provided by sense-perception. Past experience is automatically applied to present contingencies through the use of concepts. Usually concepts are associated with specific words or phrases. Vinacke suggests the following criteria for defining concepts.

(1) Concepts are not themselves sensory data but systems which are the products of our past responses to characteristic situations stimulus.

(2) Using concepts is simply applying past learning to a present situation.

(3) Concepts relate discrete sensory data.

(4) In human beings words or other symbols are the means of linking discrete items of experience.

(5) Concepts have at least two ways of functioning; the extensional use and the intensional use.

The extensional use is more or less the same for everybody who uses the concept. This use can only be defined ostensively, that is by confronting those who require a definition with an actual instance of whatever the concept refers to. 'This one' (pointing to it) 'is a rose and that one is a daffodil.' The extensional use indicates the stimulus object which the concept denotes in a direct manner.

The intensional use is liable to vary considerably from person to person. It derives from the private experience of each person who uses the concept in so far as this experience has been affected by the stimulus object. The concept of 'dog' may arouse revulsion, horror, or nausea in X, stimulate feelings of pleasure and interest in sentimental dog-lover Y, and make Z, who is a zoologist and veterinary surgeon, think in a scientifically oriented manner. X, Y, and Z all have an identical extensional use of the concept: they use the word 'dog' correctly, applying it to one type of small quadruped and withholding it from others. But intensionally the concept has a different meaning for each. Almost every concept has some intensional use determined entirely by the experience and make-up of the individual who uses it.

(6) Not all concepts are rational or even meaningful. It may be that disease is attributed to 'witchcraft' or that a horse is backed in a race because it has a 'lucky' number.

(7) Finally, concepts need not be consciously formulated. A person may respond habitually and consistently towards a particular type of stimulus situation without being able to discriminate and describe what he does or what his motive is for doing it. We do not need to be orthodox Freudians to accept this.

Concepts, then, are complex systems of higher-order responses in terms of which our more basic response-patterns are organized. The chief function of concepts is:

(1) To relate previous learning to current situations arising within the subject's present experience.

(2) To influence and organize each other. In time concepts form a complex system which can influence the course of behaviour quite independently of sensory stimulation. A word or phrase can set off a train of thought which ultimately initiates behaviour – most of the activity coming through conceptual thinking.

CONCEPT ATTAINMENT

Enough has been said to indicate what the notion of 'concept' means in psychology. How do psychologists study concepts and what do they want to find out? So far, the formation, attainment, and use of concepts have not been widely studied by psychologists. Research has been confined to two fields:

(1) How children form some of the basic concepts in terms of which logical thinking proceeds.

(2) How adult subjects who have already formed and developed a complex repertory of concepts attain new class concepts of various kinds.

Although many experiments have been carried out, some of these have been somewhat inconclusive in their results. It is true to say that serious work in tackling both concept formation and concept attainment is only just beginning.

One considerable advance in the second of these fields has been the publication of *A Study in Thinking* by J. S. Bruner and his associates, Dr J. J. Goodnow, and the late Dr G. A. Austin, all of Harvard University. For the rest of this chapter a sample of this work will be presented as an illustration of the possibilities of experimental research into the attainment of concepts. One of the most interesting features of this group of experiments is the extent to which they succeed in showing the sort of behaviour which actually goes on in conceptual activity. Indeed it is the only study in experimental psychology which does come to grips with the content of thought, with the exception of

Piaget's work with children, which is discussed in Chapter Five.

Bruner and his associates define a concept as a category, and they distinguish two sorts of category: Identity Classes, in which a variety of different stimuli are identified as the 'same' object or event; e.g. the moon sometimes appears as a thin silver crescent and sometimes as an orange circle: the child and the aged man are the same person, the same body grown old; and Equivalence Classes, in which different items are treated as equivalent for some purpose or other (our example of lettuces, tomatoes, turnips all being 'vegetables').

How are items classified according to these principles? How do we decide whether or not a particular item qualifies for membership in a specific class? We do this, Bruner suggests, by discriminating certain readily identifiable attributes and using these as the basis for classification. One learns a new concept by coming to recognize what defining attributes any X must have in order to be an instance of the concept. Thereafter one can automatically identify members of the class as soon as one discriminates one or other of the defining attributes.

What is an attribute? <u>An attribute is defined as any discriminable feature of an event which is susceptible of some variation from event to event</u>. For example, an orange may be identified in virtue of its particular colour, shape, smell, and texture. All these attributes vary from instance to instance but always within a limited range (e.g. colour varies from orange-yellow to red-orange). Within this range of variations one can use certain attributes as defining of class characteristics.

In some cases defining attributes are sensory cues – like the colour, shape, or smell of a fruit. But in other cases the attributes may be definitions or conventions established by authority or tradition. Motorists guilty of speeding in a built-up area may be defined as the class of those who travel at any speed in excess of so many m.p.h. Anyone who fits into this category is liable to prosecution at the hands of the authorities, who decide precisely what the defining attributes of 'dangerous driving' shall be.

The topic of 'attributes' is not an easy one. It requires careful treatment if we are to avoid the kind of confusions against which contemporary philosophers warn us. Fortunately the problem of what precisely a class concept is and how it is identified need not concern us. It is unquestionably the case that some class concepts are formed and identified in terms of attributes of the kind Bruner indicates, and his experiments are confined strictly to investigating this species of category or concept.

In Bruner's experiments several different kinds of category were studied. In the experiments which we are going to consider conjunctive categories only were used. Conjunctive categories are defined by the joint presence of several attributes: anything that has the properties of x, y, and z is an A (viz. all red-haired youths over six feet in height who joined the Irish Guards between January 1920 and December 1940). The attainment of a concept is simply learning a new concept and utilizing it after it has been learned. In order to acquire a new concept an existing system of concepts must be available. Concept attainment is much more a matter of modifying and adapting one's existing concepts to new uses than forming completely original concepts. Concept formation – the acquisition of new basic concepts – appears to take place in children up to the age of about fifteen years.

The chief problem in designing experiments is that of externalizing the thought processes of the subjects. Bruner's experiments succeed remarkably well in this respect. Bruner noted that if a subject has to acquire a new concept by learning its defining attributes he is really in a problem situation requiring a number of decisions. He gives the example of a stranger being shown round a town by one of its inhabitants. In the course of his introductions several citizens are pointed out as being 'influential'. The stranger is set the task of finding out what makes a man influential in this particular community. What are the attributes which define this class – wealth, occupation, educational level, age, religion? The stranger (assuming he is too shy to ask outright) has a problem. What is his task? Which attributes are relevant? How many or how few are needed for a reliable definition of 'influential'? The stranger has got to form a hypothesis as to what are the correct defining attributes and to have a method for changing it whenever it is contradicted by new evidence. Now the decisions in any concept-attainment task form a pattern. Information has to be acquired, retained, and used in a series of moves and counter-moves whose goal is the solution of the problem 'What are the defining attributes of this concept?' Such patterns, in moving towards this goal, exhibit a certain consistency and order. Bruner calls such purposive patterns of behaviour 'strategies'.

The objectives at which such strategies aim are simple:

(1) To ensure that the concept will be attained after a minimum number of encounters with relevant instances.

(2) To ensure that the concept will be attained with certainty, regardless of the number of instances one may have to test.

(3) To minimize the amount of strain on inference and memory capacities and to avoid unnecessary complications and unnecessary effort.

(4) To minimize the number of wrong categorizations and other mistakes prior to the attaining of the concept.

Such strategies need not be consciously and deliberately formulated by the subject. They are patterns of behaviour actually observed by the psychologist as he studies what his experimental subjects actually do. Behaviour conforms to strategies.

IDEAL STRATEGIES

Bruner's experimental design depends upon the following device. Partly from logical analysis of the conditions of experimental problem-situations and partly as a result of observing actual behaviour of successful problem-solvers, certain 'ideal strategies' were worked out by the experiments. These were simply the most logical and economical ways of tackling the specific problems of the experiment.

With the ideal strategies as a model, the experimenter could see in what ways exactly subjects deviate from the most perfect methods and what variables operate to account for such deviations. In this way the experiments were able to produce a detailed description of what people do when they attain concepts and what conditions influence the main shifts in behaviour.

In trying to discover what patterns the decisions of experimental subjects take and what factors influence the occurrence or cessation of any particular pattern, certain specific questions were kept in mind when designing the experiments.

(1) What does the subject think he is trying to do? How does the objective he sets up influence his strategy?

(2) What effect does the number of attributes encountered in each instance have? What is the difference between encountering instances in a random or in a systematic way? How much information must an instance carry in order to be of use?

(3) Must the subject learn each time an instance is encountered that it is an exemplar of the concept? Or is validation available only after a series of encounters?

(4) What is the cost of categorizing a specific instance wrongly and the gain from a correct categorization? How off-putting can a wrong hypothesis be under various conditions?

(5) What sorts of restrictions influence concept-attainment strategies? Pressure of time? A price to pay for testing a hypothesis?

RECEPTION STRATEGIES IN CONCEPT ATTAINMENT

Unfortunately there is not space to discuss all the experiments carried out to answer these questions. One particular set – those tackling 'Reception Strategies' will serve as a sample.

The man being shown round the strange town who was trying to find out the criteria for defining the class of 'influential citizens' had no control over the instances presented to him. Influential people were pointed out to him as and when they happened to come on the scene. This is usually the case in attaining a new concept. We have to make sense of such instances and such clues as happen to come our way. We have no control over the flow of events which contain both exemplars and non-exemplars of the concept we are trying to learn. The only control we have is that over the formation and testing of hypotheses concerning the correct defining attributes. Sound strategy in this direction is the limit of the problem-solver's freedom, and yet within these limits he can often achieve his goal with certainty.

EXPERIMENTAL DESIGN FOR RECEPTION STRATEGIES

In order to study concept attainment the following conditions must be observed:

(1) The experimenter must devise an array of instances that are alike in some respects and different in others, so that there are many ways in which instances may be grouped.

(2) The instances must be encountered by the subject in an order over which he has no control.

(3) The subject must know whether each instance is a positive or negative case in the sense of exemplifying or not exemplifying the concept chosen by the experimenter as the one the subject has to find.

(4) The subject must be given a chance to formulate and modify a hypothesis on each encounter with an instance.

The task in this experimental situation is simply that the subject is presented with a succession of exemplars and non-exemplars of a specific concept, and he has to find out what are the defining attributes of the concept. His only information is whether or not each item is an exemplar of the concept together with a thorough grounding in the purpose and materials of the experiment.

DETAILED DESIGN OF THE EXPERIMENT

Bruner used eighty-one cards. These cards had different figures and borders printed on them, and these were in different colours. There were four attributes (colour, type of figure, number of figures, and border), each with three different values as follows:

ATTRIBUTE	Colour	Type of Figure	Number of Figures	Border	
	Green	Cross	1	Single	Solid
3 Values	or Black	or Circle	or 2	or Double	or Dotted
	or Red	or Square	or 3	or Treble	or Wavy

Adapted with permission from J. S. Bruner, *A Study of Thinking*, N.Y. (John Wiley and Sons), 1956.

Examples of particular cards might be: (*a*) two red crosses with single border; (*b*) one green circle with double border.

There were 255 possible ways of grouping these cards on the basis of simple conjunctive concepts such as 'All cards with two circles' or 'All cards with red squares and two borders' or 'All black figures'.

The procedure was as follows. The task was fully described to the subject. He knew that a concept was to be defined in terms of readily discriminable visual attributes and that only certain features on the cards (border, figures, colours, etc.) were to be used as defining attributes. Only one concept was going to be selected for any given problem. He knew exactly what was required of him. His only limitations were that he did not know which concept had been selected – he had to find that out; and he was not allowed to keep a written record. After each card he was told whether or not it exemplified the concept and after each positive card he was allowed to put forward a hypothesis as to what the defining attributes were (e.g. 'Two green circles with double border').

IDEAL STRATEGIES IN THIS EXPERIMENT

What are the ideal strategies for this particular concept-attainment task?

Focusing Strategy. Bruner illustrates this strategy with the aid of a practical example. A physician examines a patient suffering from aphasia – a severe impairment of speech. He discovers that he has a damaged brain in which areas 1 to 6 are destroyed. He forms the hypothesis that the destruction of all six areas must be responsible for the symptoms of aphasia. He next meets another case with similar damage and maintains his hypothesis since the new instance confirms it. Also if he meets a negative instance (a non-aphasic with *some* or all of the areas intact) he still holds to his hypothesis. The only case which makes him change is that in which he meets a positive contradictory case, e.g. an aphasic with areas 1–3 destroyed but with 4–6 intact. When this happens he changes his hypothesis by making a compromise between the old hypothesis and the new instance. In other words, he takes what is common to these two and re-formulates his hypothesis: 'If areas 1, 2, and 3 are destroyed, then aphasia results'.

The rules for this strategy are simple:

(1) Take the first positive instance and make it (wholly and unchanged) the basis of your initial hypothesis.

(2) Then follow this schema:

	Positive Instance	Negative Instance
Confirming Instance	Maintain hypothesis	Maintain hypothesis
Contradictory Instance	Take as the next hypothesis what the old hypothesis and the present instance have in common	Impossible – unless one has misreckoned; in which case correct this from memory of past instances and present hypothesis

Adapted with permission from J. S. Bruner, *A Study of Thinking*, op. cit.

By following this procedure any subject will arrive at the correct concept on the basis of the minimum number of events encountered. The only maxims to be remembered are: (*a*) Consider what is common to your hypothesis and any contradictory instance you may meet; (*b*) ignore everything else.

The great advantage of this strategy is that it maximizes the yield of information possible at each step and also reduces strain on the subject's powers of memory and inference to a minimum. The positive instance is used as a focus and the information gained is carried forward at each step so that one's current hypothesis is a summary of what one has learned so far. The strategy is called 'focusing' for this reason, although it is also called a 'wholist' strategy, since it uses the whole of the first positive instance as a basis for hypothesis.

Scanning Strategy. This is also called 'partist' strategy, because the subject begins by framing a hypothesis about part of the initial exemplar of the concept which he encounters. He bets on some feature of the exemplar as the defining attribute. So long as further exemplars exhibit this feature he holds to his original hypothesis. Also provided non-exemplars fail to show the chosen attribute, he sticks to his choice. Should he meet a contradictory instance he changes his hypothesis by seeking a new one which is consistent with all the instances so far encountered.

The rules for following out this ideal strategy are:

(1) Begin with a feature or part of the first positive instance you encounter and use this as the basis of the hypothesis.

(2) Then follow the schema:

	Positive Instance	*Negative Instance*
Confirming	Maintain hypothesis now in force	Maintain hypothesis now in force
Contradictory	Change hypothesis and make it consistent with past instances, i.e. choose hypothesis not previously contradicted by any instance	Change hypothesis to make it consistent with past instances, i.e. choose hypothesis not previously contradicted

Adapted with permission from J. S. Bruner, *A Study of Thinking*, op. cit.

The difference between the two strategies is considerable, although either can be used to attain a concept successfully.

First, the scanning strategy makes a greater demand on memory and inference. The scanner has to fall back on memory every time he encounters a contradictory instance; whereas the focuser, if he keeps alert, need not use memory at all; the hypothesis he is using summarizes all previous encounters and their consequences for his hypothesis. Secondly, one's initial hypothesis alters considerably the probability of encountering the four different contingencies (positive or negative: confirms or contradicts the hypothesis). A mathematical analysis shows that a focuser who strictly follows the rules of this strategy will *never* encounter a negative contradictory case. It is this case which the experimental findings show to be particularly off-putting. This is a considerable advantage in helping the focus-strategist to solve his problem smoothly and quickly. The scanner, on the other hand, has to notice and memorize all the characteristics of the instances he encounters – since he may have to revise his hypothesis by scanning through the total review that has passed before him. The focuser need not spread his attention in this way.

RESULTS OF EXPERIMENTS

With these ideal strategies as a model for performance, the experimenter has at least three aims in conducting his investigation.

(1) He wants to be able to describe in what ways actual performances deviate from ideal strategies.

(2) In order to introduce variety into the task he can increase its difficulty. This can be done by altering the number of attributes in the array (e.g. the borders can be wavy, plain, or dotted, making a fifth attribute).

(3) The conditions of task attainment can be altered to see which are responsible for efficiency.

How closely do subjects adhere to one strategy or another? Are subjects consistent in their use of the focusing or the scanning strategy from problem to problem?

It is not possible to describe in detail the careful organization and control of the series of experiments or the ingenious changes introduced to discover the variables at work; some of the results of the experiments can be summarized in relation to the account here given of them.

GENERAL RESULTS

Subjects proved consistent in sticking closely to one or the other of the ideal strategies, and tended to deviate only under conditions of experimental strain. Moreover, there was a marked preference for the focusing strategy – it was adopted by 62 per cent of the total number of subjects. This result held for problem situations of varying difficulty. In other words, problem-solvers when attempting to attain a new concept by searching for defining attributes are systematic and rational in their approach; they selected strategies which conformed closely to the most logically proper method available in the circumstances. This competence on the part of the subjects seems to be general with regard to conjunctive concepts. But this is not the case with every type of class concept. Bruner and his associates carried out a series of experiments on disjunctive class concepts* in which most subjects mishandled their problems rather badly. We only mention this other experiment in order to make the point that such competence and close adherence to ideal strategy are not to be taken for granted.

The main interest of the experimenter was not so much with adherence to ideal strategy (which might have been predicted anyway) as with the particular way in which problem-solvers modify their original hypothesis in the light of whatever contingencies happen to arise in the course of the experiment. Within the framework of each strategy what tactics were adopted in meeting difficulties within the problem situation?

* See p. 83.

The Meeting and Handling of Contingencies (Focusing Strategies).
Recall the four rules for the ideal focusing strategy:

Contingency	Ideal Procedure
Positive Confirming	Maintain hypothesis
Negative Confirming	Maintain hypothesis
Positive Contradictory	Change hypothesis to whatever old hypothesis and new instance have in common
Negative Contradictory	Change hypothesis on the basis of memory of past instances

How often are these rules followed by those who begin with the 'whole' hypothesis?

Instance Encountered	% of Encounters When Ideal Rules Followed
Positive Confirming	54
Negative Confirming	61
Positive Contradictory	54
Negative Contradictory	10

The interesting result here is the rarity of the negative contradictory instance being tackled appropriately. This is probably because this is the only case in which a focusing strategist must use memory. His strategy does not require him to do so unless he misreckons – a situation which care ought to enable him to avoid. Scanners who are memory-oriented are much more successful with these cases.

It will be noticed that quite a considerable number of problem-solvers depart from the rule for handling positive contradictory contingencies. Now this contingency is met by the Intersect Rule: 'Take what is common to the old hypothesis and the contradictory positive instance'. Some subjects ignore this obvious rule and hold on to their old hypothesis. Others compromise by using only some features common to the old hypothesis and the new – a transfer over to the scanning strategy.

Another weakness displayed by some of the focusing strategists is to break the rule: 'Maintain unchanged the hypothesis if you meet a succession of positive and negative confirming instances'. These have a superstitious belief in change. It is mistakenly felt that progress cannot be maintained if one sticks to the same hypothesis.

Which of the two most important contingencies (negative confirming and positive contradictory) created most difficulty for users of this strategy?

Well, problems handled by this strategy fall into four types:
(*a*) those in which both contingencies are handled appropriately;
(*b*) those in which neither contingency is handled appropriately;
(*c*) those in which the positive contradictory instance is handled appropriately but the negative confirming is not;
(*d*) those in which the negative confirming instance is handled appropriately but the positive contradictory is not.

The results of the experiments in relation to these four possibilities are set down in the following table.

Response	*Number of Problems*	*Percentage Solved*
(a)	103	97
(b)	160	20
(c)	54	43
(d)	37	22

This table shows clearly that the handling of the Intersect Rule (viz. change hypothesis by taking what is common to the old hypothesis and its contradictory positive instance) is what is central to the focusing strategy. Handling both contingencies leads to almost certain success: handling neither to almost certain failure. If one does not handle the positive contradictory contingencies properly, failure is just as likely as if one violated both critical contingencies. It is much better to handle the negative confirming contingency ineptly, since recovery is easier in this case.

The Meeting and Handling of Contingencies (*Scanning Strategy*). How do the scanners compare when they meet the various contingencies of the experiment?

To recapitulate: The ideal strategy for scanners may be summarized in the rules:

Contingency	Ideal Procedure
(1) Positive Confirming	Maintain hypothesis
(2) Negative Confirming	Maintain hypothesis
(3) Positive Contradictory	Change to hypothesis consistent with memory of past instances
(4) Negative Contradictory	Change to the same basis as (3)

How often are these rules actually followed?

Instance Encountered	% of Encounters When Ideal Rules Followed
Positive Confirming	66
Negative Confirming	52
Positive Contradictory	50
Negative Contradictory	26

As with the focusing strategists the widest divergence from the ideal strategy comes in dealing with a negative contradictory instance. This is a very awkward contingency for the scanner – it is a 'double negative' since the card indicates what the concept is *not* and also contradicts the present hypothesis of the problem-solver. It gives no positive clue for a new hypothesis. The positive contradictory case at least provides a set of attribute values upon which a new hypothesis can be formed.

Again, following the pattern of the previously examined strategy we can illustrate how the scanners fared from the following table.

Response to Contingencies	Number of Problems	Percentage Solved
Both Appropriate	22	73
Neither Appropriate	85	8
Positive Contradictory Appropriate but Negative Confirming NOT	52	31
Negative Confirming Appropriate but Positive Contradictory NOT	29	7

Handling both contingencies brings success; handling neither brings failure. Again, if one does not handle the positive contradictory contingency appropriately, failure is as likely as if neither contingency had been adequately dealt with (8 per cent and 7 per cent successes only!).

It is obvious that the positive contradictory contingency is the crucial one for the scanner: it provides him with his basis for constructing a new hypothesis and serves as a score card against which his memory of past instances can be checked.

On the whole the scanners do not do so well as the focusers, on average over the results. This is probably due to the fact that less cognitive strain is involved in adopting the focusing strategy. Nevertheless focusers are affected by the increasing difficulty of the tasks, in a series of progressively difficult concept-attainment problems, just as much as the scanners. The situation in which focusing pays much better than scanning is one in which the pace of the experiment is cracked up by allowing only very short time-intervals between the presentation of each card and short periods only for scrutinizing each card. Sixty-three per cent of focusers are successful as compared with 31 per cent of scanners under conditions in which time-pressure is applied.

CONCLUSIONS

What is the point of these experiments? Do they tell us much about the contents and conditions of everyday thinking?

Bruner points out that his 'Reception Strategy' investigations have their limitations. The experimental situation is highly abstract and stylized – slips of cardboard with clear-cut patterns as their only attributes are not the sort of materials we normally deal with when acquiring new concepts in everyday life. Furthermore, it is rarely that in real-life concept attainment we are bombarded with a concentration of exemplars and non-exemplars, completely isolated from every other perceptual distraction, in the way in which Bruner's subjects are in the experiments. Nor indeed are we usually so well-informed about the relevant factors in a real-life situation. On the other hand, the experimental subjects lack some of the aids which we have in ordinary life when learning to make an unfamiliar classification.

In brief, real-life situations are not adequately represented by the experimental set-up: nor are they intended to be. The experiment had a specific aim which it attains in a highly successful manner, namely to pin down some of the typical sequential behaviour-patterns which subjects exhibit, and which are crucial for the accomplishment of the task, when they have to conceptualize arbitrary sequences of instances (which exemplify clearly definable class concepts on the basis of perceptually discriminable attributes). Bruner's notion of a 'strategy' has enabled him to give a comprehensive and accurate description of what the subject does and of the way in which his activities are organized in relation to his task. This has not been achieved before in any concept-attainment studies. Previous investigators had succeeded in giving a very general picture of the sort of conditions which function in concept-attainment tasks and the kind of behaviour which subjects exhibit. Bruner and his associates, through their use of the concept of 'strategies', have given a thorough description of all the relevant moves and counter-moves, the specific operations and their patterning which occur in this particular problem-situation. The 'content' of the subject's thinking as he learns a new classification is fully observed and reported. Also the conditions which affect changes in behaviour are brought to prominence in this experimental design. We know just what happens and how it happens within the experimental situation.

Other types of strategy besides 'Reception Strategies' have been investigated by Bruner and his fellow workers.

For example 'Selection Strategies' have also been studied. Using the same array of cards the subject is shown a card and told that it is an exemplar of the concept he has to discover. The total array of cards is then set before the subject on a large 'blackboard'. He can survey the lot and is allowed to pick out which he thinks are exemplars. After each choice he is told whether or not he is correct. Here the subject has control over the order in which the instances may be selected for scrutiny, although the choice of cards and their order on the board are determined by the experimenter in order to control the conditions of the experiment. For example, sixty-four cards may be displayed in eight columns and eight rows: one ordering might be randomly arranged; another might be orderly with all the cards with large black figures in the first four rows. The factors studied in this experiment are the 'selection strategies' adopted by the subject. Ideal strategies apply to the problem – how far does actual behaviour stick close to such strategies and under what conditions are deviations noted.

Disjunctive Concepts. An example of a disjunctive concept might be: 'All men qualified to vote in Drabtown Municipal elections'. The defining attributes of a voter could be several. 'Anyone over 21 years of age who resides within the town boundaries'; or 'Anyone who owns a business concern situated in the town' (even if he doesn't live in the town himself); or 'Anyone who owns property in the town' (although not necessarily either living or having business interests there). Three individuals selected at random might have no defining attributes in common with each other. How do people learn to handle disjunctive concepts? What strategies are available in learning a new disjunctive classification? Bruner's experiments revealed that all such disjunctive concepts are difficult for most subjects. These difficulties and the tactics employed to meet them make this section of Bruner's book one of the most fascinating.

Finally: since in the classification considered in the previously described studies the subjects could attain the concept with certainty, provided they could discover the defining attributes, Bruner also investigated cases in which such certainty could not be achieved. Probable cues are, indeed, often the only guide to classification. (Is that shell going to fall near here or pass overhead? Is that aircraft a friend or a foe?) Again an ingenious set of experiments resulted in an accurate description of typical operations and strategies adopted by subjects in dealing with such a set of problems.

EVALUATIONS

Bruner's work goes beyond that of any previous investigator's in scope and precision, and sets a model for future research which may be applied as it stands or with modifications. Nevertheless, his researches confine themselves to what is only part of a much wider field of conceptual behaviour – namely, the case in which a simple class concept is formed on the basis of the discrimination of certain easily identifiable attributes. There is no doubt that human beings do attain and use such class concepts in their normal thinking, and that classification, on this basis, plays an important part in the organization of perceptual data. But this is not the only type of concept which we use in our everyday thinking, nor is it even the only variety of class concept. Not all classification is based upon our ability to discriminate perceptual cues, and not every empirically grounded concept is a class concept. Yet experimental psychologists have so far limited their investigations to one variety of class concept. This means that experimental psychologists have only made a beginning – a remarkably hopeful one in the case of Bruner and his colleagues – in tackling this vast field. So far the results, however excellent, only apply to a narrow range of conceptual activity. Accordingly our knowledge of concept attainment cannot yet throw much light on 'thinking' in general.

To illustrate this point, very briefly and without rigorous analysis:

Causal Relations and Functional Properties. We learn very early in life that fire burns, bread nourishes, and knives cut. We also learn that certain different things have similar dispositions – are brittle or porous or elastic or poisonous. Now there is a sense in which we learn to clasify x, y, and z as 'brittle' or 'non-edible' or learn that all flickering-sizzling hot objects will hurt if grasped or touched.

But what is the basis of such classifications? Is it not the case that class concepts are derived from a more basic knowledge of causal relations and functional properties?

If we argue, using the classificatory device of the syllogism:

Drinking milk containing bacilli typhosus produces fever
This milk contains typhosus
This milk must not be consumed.

This may be formally stated as an AAA Figure syllogism:

All cases of milk which has bacilli are cases which produce
fever
All cases of milk in this sample are cases of milk which has
bacilli
∴ *All cases of milk in this sample are cases of milk which* ·
produces fever.

The word 'produces' implies causal knowledge, hidden in the term, so to speak. Could the argument be stated in such a way as to get rid of the notion of a causal relation altogether?

One might try to state the causal relation in the proposition:

All persons who drink milk containing bacilli are persons who
develop typhoid fever.

But what then would be the middle term in the syllogism:

All M are persons who develop typhoid fever
All persons who drink milk containing bacilli are M
∴ *All persons who drink milk containing bacilli are persons who*
develop typhoid fever.

Is a knowledge of causal relations reducible to a relation of class inclusion or class exclusion? True, we put things or events which have a common cause or a similar cause into classes (viz. the symptoms of an allergy disease are definable disjunctively: 'fur' or 'pollen' or 'pigment' produces a skin rash and rise in body temperature). But the notion of a cause is a different type of concept from that of an exemplar of a class. Causal relations enter into our interpretation of what we perceive or what is reported to us in speech or writing just as much as do simple classifications on the basis of perceptual cues. So does the grasp of dispositional properties; we may class together all the different items which display similar dispositional properties – solubility, conductivity, etc.: but we may acquire and use such concepts apart from any operations of classifying.

If classifying is one basic operation – what about serialing items (e.g. in order of increasing size: A<B<C...) or setting up correspondences? The understanding of relations is not classifying, yet it serves an analogous function and may be regarded as a conceptual activity. Also the relations between propositions of the kind axiomatized by logicians (if *p* is true, then *q* is true; either *p* or *q* is true, etc.) serve as a device for interpreting information. *A priori* reasoning is a series of operations based on various combinational systems of greater subtlety than simple classification. Yet, so far, the strategies involved in formal operations, as these are actually used in everyday thinking, have been neglected by experimental psychologists along with causal relations, dispositions, and serializing.

Neglected, that is, by all except a distinguished French psychologist, Professor Jean Piaget. Piaget, however, approaches concepts from an angle slightly different from that of the experimentalists. The American psychologists who have studied concepts – Hull, Heidbreder, Reed, and Bruner – have all confined their attention to concept attainment – the behaviour of adult subjects in modifying their repertory of existing concepts in order to learn new ones. Piaget is interested in how basic concepts originate and develop in children from birth right up to adult status. The infant has no concepts: the adult uses a complex system. In between children and adolescents have to form and develop basic concepts progressing slowly from stage to stage. How do concepts originate and change from the beginnings to maturity? In asking this question Piaget has tackled a wide range of concepts – number, space, time, morals, mortality, etc. His work, based on a variety of methods, makes a bold attempt to fill the gap which, at present, the experimentalists have left.

In the next chapter Piaget's work will be described.

It will be some time before psychologists are able to deal with the vast and complexly integrated system of concepts in terms of which a normal adult deals with his experience. So far, psychology only chips away at the fringes of this system, isolating certain simple types of concept for experimental investigation. There is a great deal of hard work to be done before a general psychological description and explanation can be given of the formation, attainment, and use of every kind of concept. Bruner's painstaking work, together with the pioneer survey of Piaget, has made a promising beginning. They have shown the sort of approach that is likely to produce results and given a clear indication of what to study. It only remains for other psychologists to set to work to fill the gaps.

SELECTED REFERENCES

Bruner, J. S., Goodnow, J. J., and Austin, G. A. *A Study of Thinking*. New York (Wiley), 1956.

Heidbreder, E. 'Toward a Dynamic Psychology of Cognition'. *Psychological Review*, 1945.

Heidbreder, E. 'The Attainment of Concepts'. *Journal of General Psychology*, 1946 and 1947.

Hull, C. L. *Quantitative Aspects of the Evolution of Concepts*. Psychological Monograph 123, 1920.

Leeper, R. 'Cognitive Processes'. Chapter 19 in Steven, S. S., *Handbook of Experimental Psychology*. New York (Wiley), 1951.

Osgood, C. E. *Method and Theory of Experimental Psychology*. Chapter 15. Oxford, 1953.

Reed, H. B. 'Factors Influencing the Learning and Retention of Concepts'. *Journal of Experimental Psychology*, 1946.

Smoke, K. L. *An Objective Study of Concept Formation*. Psychological Monograph 191, 1932.

Vinacke, W. E. *The Psychology of Thinking*. Chapter 7. New York and London (McGraw-Hill), 1952.

CHAPTER FIVE

Concept Formation in Children

THE experimental investigations of Bruner and his associates were designed to find out how new concepts are attained by adult subjects who already possess a large repertory of concepts. Indeed adults rarely form new concepts: they tend to modify existing ones to new uses. But there is a period in the life of an intelligent human being when basic concepts are formed for the first time. The study of conceptual thinking in children, especially the origin and development of basic concepts and systems, should not only show how concepts are formed but should also show what work a concept does in shaping thought.

In studying children the psychologist is faced with difficulties of the kind which bring home to him the essential problem for psychology – how to get at the data of the subject; for the methods available in child psychology are limited in scope and open to criticism. Children make poor experimental subjects, since their interest and cooperation cannot be easily sustained for long periods. The interview-questionnaire technique has to be adopted, with all its weaknesses and pitfalls. The psychologist has to get his data by talking to children and trying to get the child to think about some problem or puzzle. Or he has to arrange a demonstration (placing a jar over a lighted candle which soon extinguishes the light) and asking for an explanation. Clearly such methods are lacking in strict controls. How far does the psychologist's approach and formulation of questions influence the child's answers? To what extent does the psychologist misinterpret what the child says or does and read his own pet theories into his interpretations? Yet there are few alternatives. Experience and caution in interpreting results are the only safeguards.

The leading investigator of concept formation in children has been Professor Jean Piaget, of the Universities of Paris and Geneva. His work falls into two main phases. Between 1924 and 1937 he published some five books on the development of child thought in which he showed how radically different it is up to the age of 7 or 8 years from adult thinking – being dominated by an 'egocentric' attitude and influenced by the wishes and inner needs of the child rather than by a grasp of the environment and its properties. In the period between 1937 and the present Piaget has carried out a much more rigorous investigation into the origin and development of basic logical and mathematical concepts in children and has endeavoured to trace the growth of reasoning capacities from birth to maturity in normal European subjects.

It is impossible to discuss Piaget's recent work in the detail it merits. For one thing it involves an understanding of mathematical logic which Piaget uses as a starting-point for the construction of a new type of logic (which he calls a psycho-logic). Just as the need for explanation in physics has led to the application of pure mathematics to experimental physics and has thus given rise to mathematical physics (which attempts to construct a deductive theory to explain the experimental results), so Piaget has tried to construct a theory which applies pure logic to experimental psychology. This makes his writings highly technical. Furthermore, Piaget is a particularly difficult writer to expound. He tends to embody the results of careful observations and experiments with children in the highly systematic theory which his psycho-logic provides; it is difficult to sort out the strictly empirical contents from the abstract theory. Also he is an extremely prolific writer who is always bringing out new books and papers which modify or expand his former publications. One can only advise, 'If you want to know what Piaget has to say the only thing to do is to read Piaget himself.' It is clear that Piaget's work has yet to be completed. Only then will his contribution be evaluated and what is sound embodied in general psychology.

PIAGET'S RECENT WORK ON THE FORMATION OF LOGICAL AND MATHEMATICAL CONCEPTS

Piaget's approach is a genetic one. He attempts to distinguish levels or stages of development in the evolution of thought and to show how each stage reveals a progressive sequence from simpler to more complex levels of organization.

Piaget's starting-point is that higher psychological functions grow out of biological mechanisms.

Adaptation he defines as a balance between assimilation and accommodation which tends towards states of equilibrium (although there may be disequilibrium throughout any stage or under certain conditions even at the level of greatest maturity). 'Assimilation' is a term derived from the physico-chemical function, characteristic of every living creature, in which substances from the environment are absorbed and changed in order to sustain the organism.

At the behavioural level assimilation is the modification imposed on the environment by the activities of the organism; the organism does not remain passive towards its environment – it manipulates and changes it. Accommodation refers to the fact that the organism is changed by the action of the environment upon it. Thus a chimpanzee grasping and manipulating a wooden stick, as in Köhler's experiments, must accommodate to the size, weight, and strength of the object, and while handling the stick cannot do certain other actions. However much it assimilates – in the sense of using the stick to get food – it must accommodate itself to certain limits dictated by the situation.

Adaptation develops through a series of phases from birth to maturity. It is never quite complete, however; the equilibria achieved even in the final stages of 'maturity' tend to be unstable. In the evolution of adaptability there are many key factors, and it is these which Piaget wishes to discover and study. Two, in particular, are emphasized in his writings so far:

(1) The first of these is the extent to which an organism can control shifts of orientation. To be able to do this is *decentring* –

a concept closely related to the Gestalt psychologists' 'recentring' in problem-solving. If a baby of 9 months has a toy hidden under one of two pillows, before its eyes, it can reach for it. If the toy is then hidden under the second pillow, the infant will still keep reaching under the first. It cannot shift its orientation.

(2) The second factor is the development of operations. An operation is an action which has been 'internalized'. For example, a child learns to move beads along the wires of an abacus or to take beads from one box and place them in another. In time it learns to perform simple systematizations – to match two red beads with two blue beads and to count the units he is manipulating. He may find, at a certain stage, that no matter what ways he arranges or enumerates (counts from right to left or left to right) there is always the same result except when some are taken away or extras brought in. He can soon use words or imagery to express this sort of discovery – he is now using psychological operations instead of physical manipulations. Later he can deal with generalizations about numbers and with algebraic expressions having no concrete application, etc. But such ability derives from the internalization of such activities as combining, ordering, and putting simple objects (beads, toy soldiers, etc.) into correspondence. The child first learns to do certain actions and then is able to work out *how* it is going to do a typical action before acting. Thought originates in the interiorization of actions.

Piaget maintains that thought activities may be analysed in terms of groups or systems of such operations. Such 'groups' are relational systems which have certain defining properties. He lists five such properties:

(1) *Composition*. Any two units can be combined to produce a new unit.

(2) *Reversibility*. Two units combined may be separated again.

(3) *Associativity*. The same result may be obtained by combining units in different ways.

(4) *Identity*. Combining an element with its inverse annuls it.

(5) *Tautology*. Here the special definitions of Piaget's psycho-

logic are in evidence. In arithmetic a unit added to itself gives a new number ($1+1=2$) but repeating a logical unit only gives repetition or tautology: $A+A=A$ ('A' is an 'A' and not another thing).

We have to remember that the units are 'operations' (actions capable of being internalized, reversed, and coordinated into systems). *Reversibility* indicates that the arithmetical operation of 'addition' can be reversed by the application of 'subtraction' or that a problem-solver can return to the starting-point from which he began.

Thus an experiment might be described, using Piaget's formula, like this:

Children from 5 to 8 years are shown an open box containing 20 wooden beads. Call this class of 20 beads 'B'. Most of the beads are brown (class A) but some are white (class A^1). Therefore $B=A+A^1$.* The children are asked: 'Are there more brown beads in the box or more wooden beads?' – a catch question! The ability to answer this simple question depends on the grasping of a simple relation of class inclusion between two classes.

$A<B=$'the part A is smaller than its whole B.' A child between 5 and 7 years cannot usually achieve this grasping of the principle. He says 'There are more brown beads (A) than wooden beads (B) because there are only a few white ones (A^1)'. The child finds it difficult to reason about the whole and its parts at the same time: if he concentrates on the whole he loses sight of the parts, and vice versa. The child of 7–8 years can usually answer the question – he can perform operations of composition or decomposition of the units involved.

$B=A+A^1$, therefore $A=B-A^1$ and $A^1=B-A$, hence $A<B$.

The *reversible* actions of composing and decomposing units into classes are the basis for understanding the logical relationships.

Piaget's main interest is to show how simple operations can be ordered or coordinated in terms of systems or groups and

---

* This may be interpreted: place all the beads together, being equivalent to taking the brown beads and adding the white beads to form one class out of two.

how such groups are discernible in the activities of children. This is not to say that the children are consciously aware of these systems, but merely that their activities are governed by such principles. The 8-year-old child who solves the puzzle question is not aware of the principles he follows in composing or decomposing the class B into A and A^1, and working out how the browns and the whites are related as parts of a whole: he just actively *does* work this out. The psycho-logical formulae (A, B, $+$, $-$, $=$, etc.) merely formalize the operations actually performed. They describe the concepts attained, at the particular stage of development under review, and show how these concepts are employed.

THE DEVELOPMENT OF OPERATIONS

Operations are thus actions. They are internalizable since they can be carried out symbolically without losing their character as actions. They are reversible, e.g. the operation of combining x and y can be reversed by separating y from x in the way that a habit, like reciting the alphabet from A to Z, cannot be reversed without a new habit having to be learned first. And they are capable of being coordinated into systems since they cannot exist in isolation from other operations. One can only understand that A is less than B because one understands the serial operation $A<B<C<D$ ... just as one can only classify an object if one is familiar with various classificatory systems. Operations and their groupings are the main object of Piaget's developmental approach to concept formation. He has carried out innumerable tests and experiments with children of different age-groups, and as a result he distinguishes five main phases or stages in the growth of concepts. Not every child follows these stages in its individual growth – the bright child achieves a particular level earlier than the average child, and the dull child fails to reach the final stages of maturity. The average pattern of development follows his scheme and all children pass through each of the phases in turn – except the dull ones. What is this pilgrim's progress?

The Sensori-Motor Period (Birth to 2 years). In this phase the infant can perform only motor actions – manipulating objects in trial and error fashion. But some beginnings of intelligent behaviour are observable. For instance, a child may draw a coverlet towards it in order to grab a toy lying on the surface.

However, there are no operations since the child cannot yet internalize its activities. The child begins, however, to form concepts of 'objects'. It learns to construct the notion of a permanent object lying beyond the range of immediate perception. At first a child will reach for and grasp a watch placed within its field of vision but will lose all interest if the watch is covered up. Soon it learns to remove the cloth and to search behind a screen for toys hidden there. At first he will tend to look always in the same place for hidden objects but gradually acquires the capacity to search in unfamiliar positions. This development – the formation of the behavioural concept of permanent objects (not necessarily regarded as belonging to an external world) results from the organization of a spatial field which is in turn a by-product of the increasingly effective coordination of the child's bodily movements. There are the beginnings of reversibility (the ability to go back to a starting-point) and associativity (the ability to change movements) – although these are very 'embryonic'. Even at the sensori-motor stage in which sense-perception and movement become increasingly coordinated, there is intelligence displayed in the factors of reversibility and conservation. Much of what is acquired at this stage, as at all stages, is foundational and is carried forward for further development in the succeeding stages.

Pre-Operational Thought (2 to 4 years). Children learn the trick of imitation. They can feign sleep and indulge in other forms of 'representative imitation', often deferring the imitation until some time after the original event. The internalization of imitated actions is the basis for imagery. This move is the beginning of symbolic behaviour. The internalized action can be used to stand for something other than itself. This, in turn, leads to the understanding of signs – the learning of language. Out of the general 'symbolic function' speech begins. If a child in this age-group is asked 'Where is the hammer?' it will move an arm up and down and proceed to look in the tool-box. But words are tied to actions or to needs; the child has to accommodate to the use of words by adults – it does not develop their use independently of social training. Moreover, its words are used in a very rough and ready fashion, as when 'Pussy' is applied to dogs, rabbits, and even to any moving or bouncing thing. Naming seems to be the first step in adapting to language since concrete permanent objects are vaguely discriminated and recognized.

The phase is dominated by an egocentric attitude in which the sign used to indicate an object or event is confused with the thing signified and an incapacity to distinguish between inner experiences and external factors. Objects such as dolls, stones, the sun, clouds, etc., are also treated as living and endowed with intentions and desires. Yet thought has begun in the invention and use of symbols to represent absent objects and happenings and in the response to signs.

Intuitive Thought (4 to 7 years). It is much more difficult to reproduce actions in thought than to carry them out behaviourally. Operations, in the technical sense, develop slowly. There is an absence of both reversible operations and the concept of conservation except at the sensori-motor level. Intelligent behaviour tends to be limited to overt actions and the thinking of children in this phase is tied to perceptual factors.

The characteristic achievements and limitations of this phase are well illustrated by certain experiments with children. The subject is presented with two glass phials, A_1 and A_2, both identical in size and shape. He fills each glass with beads, putting one bead in A_1 and one bead in A_2 and so on, and readily admits that there is an equal number of beads in each glass. If a differently shaped glass B is now taken and A_2 is emptied into it, the child will assert that the quantity of beads has changed, even when he knows that none has been added or removed. If the glass B is tall and slender he tends to argue either that there are more beads now than before since it is taller or that there are fewer beads because it is thinner. His reasoning is dominated by the prominent perceptual feature – the height or width of the new glass. Instead of realizing that these two factors are inter-dependent and concentrating on the conservation of the quantity of beads he is misled by one or other of the two new percept-ually dominant features. There are, however, intuitive 'centralizations' and 'decentralizations'. If the child asserts that there are more beads in the B glass because the level has been raised he is centring on the relative heights in B and A_2 but ignoring the relevant factor of width. If the beads are poured from B into still taller and thinner glasses a point is reached at which the child argues that there are now fewer beads because the container is too narrow. He has decentred his focus from height to width as a relevant factor. It is his failure to relate the two factors and deduce conservation which shows the limits of this intuitive grasp of the perceptual configuration and what is relevant to the problem. These limits, Piaget thinks, arise from the fact that intuitive thought is essentially the imaginary representation of complex configurations. Since the child cannot go beyond these, the relations it constructs can be neither combined nor reversed: each centring distorts or destroys others which ought to be re-lated in order to construct the 'grouping' of operations required for the solution of the problem. The subject cannot grasp the problem as a whole. He is too involved with present action and sense-content.

Nevertheless this phase involves a progress towards reversi-bility, one of the most essential conditions in the development of operations. Each distortion, when carried to an extreme, forces the subject to return to relations he has ignored – as in the case of the phials which get taller and thinner throughout the course of the experiment. Every decentralization of an intuitive grasp of the configuration makes a move towards the concept of conservation, attained through the coordination of different 'views' of the situation.

Concept Formation in Children

Concrete Operations (8 to 11 years). In this phase the actions of combining, dissociating, ordering, and setting up correspondences become 'grouped': they become capable of deliberate reversal. Although still concerned with actual operations carried out on concrete objects, classification and qualitative seriation are mastered.

One of the first systems or groups to emerge is that of classification, the inclusion of one class within another.

Another operation is that of seriation or the forming of simple asymmetrical relations into a system. This capacity is illustrated in the following experiment.

If a child is given a number of rods which are unequal in length (A, B, C, D, etc.) and is required to arrange them in order of increasing length, and further if it is fixed that the variation in length is small so that the rods have to be compared two at a time, then it will be found: (*a*) that before the age of 7 children work unsystematically, comparing pairs (e.g. BD, AE, CG) and then correcting the results. But (*b*) after 7 children work systematically. The older children select the smallest stick first and then the smallest which is left and so on. This involves the coordination of two relations: $A<B+B<C=A<C$.

These operations at the concrete level mark an improvement on intuitive thought. The subject is no longer tied to particular states of the object and is able to coordinate separate 'viewpoints' of the situation into a system. Such groupings attain, for the first time, an equilibrium between the assimilation of objects to the child's action and the accommodation of its ideas to modifications in the objective situation.

Transitive relations are grasped which make simple deductions possible: $A=B$ and $B=C \therefore A=C$, or $A<B$ and $B<C \therefore A<C$. As soon as these additive groupings are mastered, the child can grasp multiplicative groupings in the form of correspondences. Once he can serialize one set $A_1<B_1<C_1 \ldots$ it is easy to serialize another set $A_2<B_2<C_2$ which corresponds to the first, term for term.

Moreover, this gives rise to the concept of number. If a child under 6 is presented with two rows of counters he can make them numerically equal only by spacing out the two rows with each counter opposite a corresponding member: he cannot recognize the invariance of number independently of such spatial arrangement. How then does the concept of number emerge? First the child has learned to establish a one-to-one correspondence involving the conservation of equivalence in spite of qualitative differences (the beads or counters may be of different shapes or colours). Now, given the additive groupings of classification and the serialization of asymmetrical relations, if the child can combine these two operations so that the unit is treated both as an element in a class (1 included in 2, 2 in 3) and also as a member of a series (the first unit preceding the second one, etc.) he has all he needs to form the concept of a number. Now he can grasp the operation of numerical succession: $n+1$, viz. the simple repetition of unity: $1+1=2$, $2+1=3$, etc. So long as the child concentrates on the individual elements with all their diversity (beads, toy soldiers, etc.) he can either combine them according to equivalent attributes (constructing classes) or arrange them according to their differences (constructing asymmetrical relations). What he cannot do is to treat them as equivalent and different simultaneously. Number, once it emerges at this concrete level, is simply a collection of objects regarded as both equivalent and orderable – the only difference between each being reduced to their particular position in a series. It is this transition, Piaget holds, the ignoring of qualitative differences and the *combining* of difference with equivalence that marks the beginning of mathematical concepts. This happens simultaneously with the development of classification and seriation. Classes, relations, and numbers all appear in thought together at roughly the same time.

Other operations appear at this stage. The concepts of space, time, and the material world are formed. This is not surprising, since joining objects into classes and classes within classes has some affinity with joining parts into a whole and configurations into greater complexes; seriation, expressing differences, is the basis for relations of ordering or placing-displacing, and number makes possible the operation of measuring.

At the age of 8 children coordinate relations of temporal order (before-after) with duration (longer as compared with shorter lengths of time). Previously these two were kept separate and unrelated. Now they are combined and activities are related temporally, in the common-sense manner, for the first time. Again the notion of a common space, based on the coordination of operations hitherto developed independently, begins to form – the child can believe that lengths and areas remain constant however much perceptual data change, and use systems of perspective, sections, etc.

The construction of related groupings thus marks a big step forward in the growth of intelligence. But it must be emphasized that these operations are not yet logical operations. They are only mastered in *concrete* situations where the child is actively manipulating material data which he can see, touch, and fixate. If we make the child reason with verbal propositions he is often completely incapable of handling abstractly the very operations which he controls quite easily when they are applied to concrete situations. Action is given a logical, coherent structure by concrete operations, but these do not succeed at this stage in spreading to thought activities. Formal operations which are not embedded in perceptual situations have not developed at this stage.

The limitations to which concrete operations are subject are illustrated by the following problem. Two lumps of modelling clay of similar size and weight are shaped like pancakes. One of these is re-modelled in a sausage-like form and various groups of children are asked what changes have taken place in the altered lump of clay. Three problems are put:

(1) Does the altered lump still contain the same quantity of clay as the unaltered lump?

(2) Does it still have the same weight?

(3) Does it still have the same volume – would it still displace the same quantity of liquid?

In the pre-operational phases (2 to 4 years) children think that because the shape has changed therefore size, weight, and volume all change as well. ('There is more clay now than there was before since the thing is longer.')

In the 7–8 years period children recognize that it has only changed shape and that it can be easily restored to its former appearance without change in the amount of substance – but they cannot accept conservation of weight.

Towards 9–10 years children admit conservation of weight as well as that of substance, but they deny conservation of volume. They now recognize that what the object has gained in length it has lost in thickness, but cannot apply a third variable. Only at about 11–12 years do children accept the conservation of all three attributes – this achievement taking nearly five years to develop.

It is the case that various aspects of the physical world are given structure by a group of concrete operations which results in the intelligent use of invariants, viz. concepts of conservation. But these concrete operations are not generalized simultaneously to all possible fields of application. This is because concrete operations have not yet been formalized into a system of general principles – they are still tied to bits of concrete behaviour. The next phase of development requires a 'structured whole' in which various operations and groups are interrelated on the basis of more general principles – formal or logical principles proper.

Propositional or Formal Operations (11 to 14 years). The attainment of logical operations comes with adolescence. Concrete groupings are transposed to a new level. Whereas the children in the previous four phases are concerned with sensori-motor activities or concrete operations, the adolescent thinks beyond present tasks and forms theories. Hypotheses are formed and experimented with. The older youth makes assumptions and proceeds to draw conclusions which are not directly related to present factors. He may act on what he takes to be valid inferences and is interested in testing inferences. For example, when presented with metal balls of different weights and masses on a horizontal plane, and set the problem of explaining motion, adolescents will take statements r and s, which state facts about friction and air resistance, and p, which expresses the fact that the balls have come to rest, and reason thus:

$$p > (q \lor r \lor s \lor \ \dots \ )$$

from which $(q, \bar{r}, s\dots) > \bar{p}$ (its contrapositive). This formula is to be interpreted as deducing that without the intervention of those factors which cause the balls to come to a standstill (their absence being symbolized by $\bar{q}, \bar{r}, \bar{s}\dots$) the movement of the balls would continue indefinitely $(\bar{p})$; which is a form of the principle of inertia. This is the application of J. S. Mill's principle of the 'method of difference', which varies one factor at a time while the rest are kept constant.

What the adolescents are doing in solving this problem is to deal with statements or propositions as well as with events. They are performing operations with statements, and this involves logical operations of the kind: if p is true, then q is true ($p > q$ or implication); either p is true, or q is true ($p \lor q$ or disjunction); p and q cannot both be true (p/q or incompatibility), etc. This is a new kind of reasoning which develops out of the operations and groupings acquired at the former concrete level.

Thus if we regard reasoning about things and events as first-order groupings of operations, operating upon these operations or their results is a second-order grouping of operations. The first-order grouping involves the combination, reversal, etc., of concrete operations. The second-order grouping gives rise to new relations of a logical kind (implication, contradiction, etc.), which hold between *statements*. These statements are derived from classifications, seriations, and other operations which are formed and developed at the concrete level.

Nor is the construction of logical or propositional operations the only achievement of this final stage. A new group of operations emerges which Piaget calls 'operational schemata'.

The first of these deals with combinational operations (combinations, permutations, aggregations). This acquisition is illustrated by an experiment in which boys of 12 to 14 years were given five colourless and odourless liquids of different chemical composition. Three of these gave a coloured product when mixed with certain of the others, one removed the colour so produced, and the fifth was neutral. At this level the subjects worked systematically to combine the liquids in all possible ways.

Other schemata concern proportions, mechanical equilibria, probabilities, correlations, and multiplicative compensations. All of these are worked out and applied in experimental situations without previous school training in mathematics or physics by children of this age-group. It should be emphasized that these logical operations are exhibited in the actual behaviour of the subjects – their reasoning follows the principles which logicians express in their formulae, although the children concerned do not yet understand these principles. They are completely unfamiliar with the laws of logic or the principles of mathematics. What they achieve at this stage is the capacity to *think* logically and *do* mathematics. A still higher level of abstract thinking is needed in order to comprehend *what it is* to reason properly.

What Piaget is concerned with is describing the way in which logical and mathematical relationships are discovered and used through the coordination and systematizing of operations. A logician seeks to justify certain procedures by axiomatizing these characteristic operations and showing what rules fallacies are breaches of. The logician's job is to exhibit the rules which sound reasoning must follow if it is to reach true or probable conclusions. Piaget's psycho-logic is designed to provide an adequate description of what logical structures are actually exhibited embedded in actual behaviour at different levels of development. His researches suggest that logical and mathematical thinking grows step by step from the sensori-motor behaviour of the infant to the controlled and systematic handling of operations of the concrete operational and formal operational stages.

The final phase leads to two sorts of acquisitions which are the basis of reasoning of an adult kind.

(1) Logical or propositional operations are formed which constitute a self-contained system independent of any concrete contents and which also serve as a means of coordinating operations acquired at earlier stages into a single system.

(2) There also emerges a series of operational schemata which have no direct connexion with each other but which contribute towards the grasping of the relationships studied in the natural sciences.

THE PROGRESSIVE DIFFERENTIATION OF OPERATIONS

There is thus a progress from one level of adaptation to the next. The important stages for the development of thought are the last three.

(1) The intuitive stage is the one in which the child begins to represent absent objects through the use of signs. Not only are things and happenings which are not perceptually here and now envisaged, but the child can understand means-end relationships and work out what it has to do to realize its wants and needs (e.g. to get sweets out of a cupboard). The child has a sort of map of reality, but it has many blank spaces, and he has not mastered sufficient coordinations to deal with more than a few limited situations. He has not yet formed the concepts of class or relations because actual perceptual configurations or represented spatial configurations in imagination are his only data.

(2) Between 7 and 8 years clear-cut operations are formed: concepts of classes, relations, and numbers, and ideas of space, time, and a material world in which everything has its place in relation to everything else, emerge for the first time. But there are limits on the extent to which the environment can be understood.

(3) Finally there is the differentiation of operations tied to actions from logical operations concerned with the relation between statements expressing operations. Possibilities as distinct

from 'hard facts' can be dealt with and the world of experience analysed and manipulated in ways hitherto impossible.

Thus logical, mathematical, and physical concepts which are basic to any reasoning grow out of simple overt activities such as classifying, serializing, or enumerating beads or toy soldiers. The key concepts in terms of which Piaget describes this development are those of 'operations' and 'groupings' and the merit of these technical terms cannot be appreciated without going into the Piaget 'psycho-logic' in some detail; an enterprise beyond the scope of this elementary treatment of his findings. Anyone who reads his own summary in *Logic and Psychology*,* from which much of the material for this chapter has been taken, will see how Piaget is able to pin down the precise structure of any given operation as it appears embedded in the actual behaviour of his subjects in various experimental situations. He is able to describe how logical thinking grows bit by bit from one stage of adaptation to the next and in so doing he has laid the foundation for many more minute investigations into the origin and growth of basic concepts in human thought.

CONCLUSIONS

It will be noted that there is some affinity between Piaget's concept of 'groupings' (which he defines as systems fulfilling certain conditions of reversibility, composition, etc.) and Bruner's concept of 'strategies' which are used to describe the sequential patterning which an adult subject's decisions take when he is attempting to attain a new concept. Both of these concepts are intended to model the structure of actual thought processes, neglecting certain incidental features and fixating what is crucial. Bruner begins where Piaget leaves off – with mature adults who have mastered all the basic operations and groupments necessary for thought. Moreover, Bruner concentrates on a narrow front; he attempts to study only one species of conceptual thinking, namely categorizing on the basis of discriminable attributes. Piaget, on the other hand, ranges widely over the entire field of

* Piaget, J., Manchester University Press, 1953.

conceptual activity from the forming of the notion of concrete permanent objects persisting beyond the range of the subject's perceptual field to the concepts of space, time, number. How far have such studies taken us in the understanding of concepts and their role in thinking?

The answer would seem to be that, so far, psychologists have made a good beginning in studying concept formation and concept attainment. They have succeeded in showing that there is a possibility of tracking down what happens when concepts are being acquired – showing how their subjects are behaving and what conditions appear to influence what they do. But it is only a beginning. Piaget has carried out what is the first systematic survey of the field as a whole from the genetic approach, and Bruner has devised ingenious experiments for giving a more accurate description of typical concept-attainment activities with regard to one kind of concept. But the greater part of this vast and complex aspect of human behaviour remains to be explored more thoroughly. This can only be achieved after many specific investigations have been carried out in order to discover in detail what people actually do when thinking conceptually.

As Vinacke has pointed out, there are many quite different problems for the psychologist. Firstly he has to find out how human beings have this ability for conceptual thought. Piaget has already thrown out brilliant suggestions concerning the way in which concepts develop out of simpler behaviour patterns, but the details have still to be filled in and many of his hypotheses more rigorously tested. Secondly, Piaget's lead in studying the formation of the basic repertory of concepts has to be followed up. Thirdly, the way in which specific concepts are attained both in children and at the mature adult level presents an almost endless series of research projects concerning every conceivable type of concept – not merely logical, mathematical, or physical concepts, but those found in the discourse of art, religion, politics, social relationships (e.g. those concerning manners, tastes, customs, traditions). So far, psychologists have only carried out preliminary reconnaissance; the main attacks have yet to be planned and undertaken. Finally there is the point that, so far, psychologists seem to have concentrated on the acquisition of concepts. But in everyday life we use a complex universe of concepts without having to form new ones or even attain modifications of any specific concepts already formed. We interpret what we see and hear or what is reported to us in speech or writing in terms of our already-established repertory. How does this repertory function as a complex whole? It clearly helps us to deal with our environment and the problems arising from our assimilation of it: but in what ways do psychological factors in conceptual thinking operate so as to render our adaptations inefficient? Contemporary philosophers have argued persuasively that much confused and muddled thinking – in which we get hopelessly bogged down, or trapped in blind alleys or spinning round in circles – is due to the misuse of the concepts in terms of which we fixate and proceed to consider our situation. It is true that by 'concepts' philosophers mean words or phrases which are ambiguous or vague in meaning. But the psychologists' use of the term 'concept', in which it refers to a psychological operation, has some affinity with the philosophers' in this context. An inappropriate or mishandled concept clearly hinders successful adaptation. One line of investigation in the study of concepts must therefore be directed upon the application and misapplication of established systems of concepts during intelligent behaviour, although it is not easy to conceive how to investigate such a complex state of affairs using genuinely experimental methods.

One of the criticisms directed against Piaget is that his researches into the origin and development of thought in children do not pay sufficient attention to the factor of learning. Quite apart from the development of the kind of operations which he studies, children acquire the capacity to learn. They have to learn how to learn, and their success results in all kinds of habits, skills, and abilities. Many typical learning operations and their products obviously play a considerable part in problem-solving and in concept attainment. Even perception involves learning, since the muscular movements of the eyes have to be gradually corrected until certain features of a stimulus are discriminated and others rendered peripheral. Learning is one of the most fundamental variables in any psychological discussion.

Chapter Six will introduce the general topic of learning operations both as a basis for illuminating what has already been discussed and as a preparation for the discussion on the influence of language upon thought.

SELECTED REFERENCES

Bruner, J. S. Review article on *The Growth of Logical Thinking* in *British Journal of Psychology*, November 1959.

Mays, W. 'The Epistemology of Professor Piaget'. *Proceedings of the Aristotelian Society*, 1953–4.

Mays, W. 'Development of Logical and Mathematical Concepts: Piaget's recent Psycho-Logical Studies'. *Nature*, Vol. 174, October 1954.

Parsons, C. Review article on *The Growth of Logical Thinking* in *British Journal of Psychology*, February 1960.

Piaget, J. *Logic and Psychology*. Manchester University Press, 1953.

Piaget, J. *The Psychology of Intelligence*. London (Routledge), 1950.

Piaget, J. *The Child's Conception of Number*. London (Routledge), 1952.

Piaget, J., and Inhelder, B. *The Growth of Logical Thinking*. London (Routledge), 1958.

Scheerer, M. 'Cognitive Theory' in *Handbook of Social Psychology*, Chapter 3. Edited by G. Lindzey. Cambridge (Mass.) (Addison-Wesley), 1954.

Vinacke, W. E. *The Psychology of Thinking*, Chapter 9. New York and London (McGraw-Hill), 1952.

CHAPTER SIX

Learning Operations

ANY mature living creature brings to a situation in which it is active a whole repertory of previously acquired habits and dispositions. In the case of intelligent human behaviour, part of what we mean by calling it 'intelligent' is to refer to the fact that such activity depends upon prior learning. Learning is, therefore, one of the necessary conditions for thinking to take place.

It is not easy to define 'learning'. Learning, it is often suggested, is any change in the general activity of an organism the effects of which persist and recur over a period of time and which are strengthened by repetition or practice. This simple definition at least distinguishes changes produced by learning from changes which result from other causes – such as the maturation process (the natural development of the organism).

Learning usually takes place when the existing repertory of responses has to be modified in order that a successful adaptation is made in a new situation. What constitutes 'success' or 'failure' in such circumstances is largely dependent upon the motivational state of the organism at the time. Motives will be discussed in relation to thinking in some detail later, in Chapter Eight. For the present it is sufficient for our purpose to think of a motive in terms of a specific goal which has to be reached by some overt adaptive behaviour. For example, if an animal is hungry it must search for, secure, and consume food in order to satisfy its need: if a human being needs approval and acceptance he must do something which will evoke praise from other people. Success, in this context, is the attainment of a goal through appropriate behaviour. Learning is usually a change in performance initiated by a motive and requiring some new organization among established habits, skills, and tendencies.

We are all familiar with examples of living creatures exhibiting the capacity to learn. But how do living things acquire the ability to learn? And how do learning mechanisms operate in controlling overt behaviour? There is, unfortunately, no more complicated or controversial topic in psychology than learning theory. It is only in order to indicate the importance of learning operations as one of the essential conditions which influence thought processes that the subject has to be treated in this book. The treatment will be elementary, but however much it is simplified the discussion cannot avoid a certain inherent complexity. It is essential to pay close attention to the facts of learning. The reason for this is fairly obvious. In a narrow sense of the word learning can be contrasted with 'reasoning' or 'thinking': in a broader sense of the term it can be maintained that reasoning is merely a complicated form of learning. There is a continuous development from simple learning operations to the application and modification of prior learning, in a problem-solving situation, which simply is a kind of 'thinking'. It is impossible to discuss thinking without including a discussion on the nature and function of learning.

What follows, in this chapter, is an account of the simple types of learning operations, with an attempt to show how these grow into more complex patterns of behaviour which in turn constitute recognizable conditions of typical problem-solving processes. The discussion issues from the simple situation in which an organism produces the correct or successful response for the first time in an unfamiliar, non-routine situation. This elementary fact leads the psychologist to consider two questions:

(1) How does this new successful response emerge for the first time in an unfamiliar situation? Since the situation is unfamiliar and the subject has never produced just this particular pattern of behaviour before, it is not inconceivable that the correct response might never come, or come only after many blind attempts. But it does come, and quite quickly and smoothly in case after case. Why does this happen?

(2) Once the correct response is achieved, how does it persist and reappear when the occasion demands it? Responses do *not* have to be acquired over and over again: the subject can reproduce the new trick and even modify it to fit variations in the context. How do such modifications become semi-permanent or permanent?

These two questions dominate investigations into the basic factors involved in learning. Let us consider simple learning, the simplest we know anything about.

CONDITIONING

At the beginning of the century, the Russian physiologist Pavlov was investigating glandular secretions in digestion and was using dogs as his experimental subjects. He noticed that almost any stimulus which preceded the actual arrival of food – the footsteps of the person bringing the food, the smell of the food, the sight of the food container – was sufficient to elicit the salivation response in the mouth of the dog. Now, the 'natural' stimulus to salivation is the smell, sight, and taste of the food in the mouth; therefore, in this case, an entirely 'artificial' or secondary stimulus was setting off the food-taking reaction.

Pavlov analysed the relationship between stimulus and response in this case as follows. Seeing, smelling, tasting food (Stimulus S_1) originally sets off the response of salivating (R). S_1 is the unconditional stimulus (symbolized hereafter by US) and the response in this case is the unconditional response UR. Now a second stimulus (S_2), the sounding of a buzzer is presented, either simultaneously with or immediately before S_1. If this pairing of S_1 and S_2 is repeated many times, S_2 will come by itself to elicit the salivation. S_2 is then called the conditional stimulus (CS) and the reaction once associated thus with S_2, becomes a conditional response (CR). The reaction has become conditioned to a new stimulus (S_2). This process of conditioning is a simple type of learning; one of the simplest so far discovered by experimental psychologists.

Although this type of learning occurs in many experimental

studies it is not easy to detect it in real-life situations. This is partly because, as a very simple learning operation, it is overlaid by more complex responses, and partly because simple conditioning, in the strictest sense, only works in situations in which incidental stimuli do not interfere with the association between S_1 and S_2. Also, in real life, it is difficult to judge which stimuli are the ones to which a subject is responding; the most obvious source of stimulation to an observer may not be actively affecting the subject.

Nevertheless many habits have this origin in the association of a previous neutral stimulus with an unconditional stimulus, and more complex forms of learning appear to exhibit the patterns which are clearly apparent for conditioning.

Reinforcement. The US is usually strongly associated with the unconditional response (UR). Thus the unconditional *reflex* may be innate or be established early in life. The CR, however, is not well established. It has got to get started somehow and then become strengthened. How does this come about?

Presumably from the subject's point of view the CS is something which arises fortuitously in experience: then it just happens that is certain situations the US and the CS come together. Temporal contiguity is the basis of the new association and also of its strengthening. The S_1–R reinforces the S_2–R relationship through the S_1–S_2 relationship. The notion of reinforcement is important for learning theory. 'Reinforcement' merely refers to the fact that certain stimuli increase the strength and persistence of a response when presented in close temporal conjunction with the response. The strength of the response can be assessed approximately by choosing one of several possible indices, e.g. in the example under consideration the amount of salivation in the dog's mouth. Pavlov summarizes this in his First Law: 'The occurrence of an unconditional reflex in temporal contiguity with a conditional reflex increases the strength of the latter.' Another of Pavlov's 'Laws of Conditioning' asserted:

'If a conditioned reflex is elicited without reinforcement by an unconditional reflex, the conditional reflex is weakened or inactivated.'

For the new response to persist it must be followed immediately by the US or else it tends to weaken towards extinction. Reinforcement – at least in this Pavlovian sense of the US having to back the CS – is necessary for learning. There are other meanings given to reinforcement by other learning theorists (viz. Hull), but there is no need for us to get entangled in the controversies of learning theory here. In Pavlov's experiments the presentation of the US is not dependent upon the animal subject making any particular response. The CR (the buzzer followed by salivation) is reinforced by the UR (food followed by salivation). There is a variety of conditioning which involves the presentation of the US only when a correct response is made by the subject: this is called 'Instrumental Learning'.

INSTRUMENTAL LEARNING

In Pavlov's conditioning experiment, in which a dog learns to transfer the response to food to the buzzer, this is brought about by giving food whether or not the dog makes any response to the buzzer during the acquisition phase. In instrumental conditioning the response to be learned must occur *before* reinforcement occurs. The learned response is instrumental in securing the reinforcement and the reinforcement acts as a sort of 're-ward'. An example may be taken from an experiment by B. F. Skinner.

Skinner placed a rat in a puzzle box containing a food-tray which receives a pellet of food only if the rat learns to press a lever situated beside the tray. The rat is hungry and restless; it accidently presses the lever – a probable event: a pellet appears which the rat eats. The rat remains near the tray and soon makes the lever-pressing action a second time. It does not take long for the rat to press the lever whenever it is hungry. Pressing the lever (CR) causes the food pellet to appear (US). The eating of the food is the UR. The CS is probably the sight or smell of the lever – or the entire complex of stimuli associated with the experiment. The two experiments may be illustrated:

Pavlov:

$$CS - US - UR$$
Buzzer Food Saliva
leading to $CS - CR - US - UR$
Buzzer Saliva Food Saliva
R_1

Skinner:

$$CS - R_2 - US - UR$$
Sight of Lever R_3 Food Eating
Pressing
Lever
leading to $CS - CR - US - UR$
Lever Pressing Food Eating
Lever

Figure 7

The differences between the two types of simple learning operation should be obvious from the diagrams.

In classical conditioning (Pavlov) the responses (salivating) are similar although not identical (amount and rate of salivation differs), whereas in instrumental learning the responses are dissimilar (e.g. eating compared with pressing a lever).

In instrumental learning the US appears only after a series of actions which constitute what has been learned: in Pavlovian conditioning the US is there from the beginning and the subject has to learn to transfer the response from the US to the CS.

Yet the 'laws' of acquisition and extinction of responses follow the same pattern in each case. Both are a form of 'conditioning' in which differing means produce a similar result.

The Development of Simple Learning. There are many topics which could be discussed in connexion with simple learning operations, e.g. the problem of how established responses are weakened and extinguished. It is necessary to move on and consider how simple learning develops into more complex forms.

The first complication is that of height-order conditioning.

For example, a dog may be presented with food as US and then conditioned to salivate to a buzzer. The buzzer comes to

113

elicit salivation when presented without the food. If a light is now presented with the buzzer, this new stimulus may itself come to elicit salivation, although it has never been directly associated with the food. W. C. Shipley reports an interesting experiment. He paired a faint light with a sudden tap on the cheek. This latter stimulus elicited winking (an unconditional reflex). The tap was then paired with an electric shock to the finger which elicited withdrawal movement of the finger. Later the flash of light, which had never been paired with the shock, evoked the finger flexion.

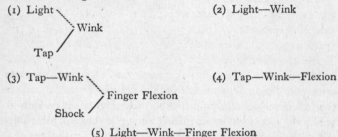

(1) Light⟍

　　　⟍Wink

　Tap⟋

(2) Light—Wink

(3) Tap—Wink⟍

　　　⟍Finger Flexion

　Shock⟋

(4) Tap—Wink—Flexion

(5) Light—Wink—Finger Flexion

Figure 8

What happens is that in (4) and (5) the finger movement becomes attached not directly to the tap on the cheek, but to the response (winking) which is made to the tap (as in 4). This is the second conditioning. In the first conditioning, the light comes to elicit winking (1 and 2). Thus through the mediating link of the winking response, the light comes to evoke the finger flexion – even when the light has never been directly paired with the tap (the US for the finger flexion). The wink helps to switch the finger flexion response from one stimulus to another. It acts as a mediating response between two separate conditionings and so produces a new learning sequence. This is a simple specimen of how complex conditionings begin to develop.

What results from the elaboration of conditioning is the formation of a complex hierarchy of habits. The concept of 'habit' is not a precise one. Nevertheless it is useful. Habits vary from being specimens of Pavlovian conditioning to much more complex behaviour sequences. When we describe X as a 'capable and conscientious' student we refer summarily to a complicated hierarchy of habits – regular attendance at classes, attention in class, care and application in reading and writing exercises, persistence in devoting time and energy to work and in limiting leisure, and regularity in high-scoring performances in comparison with other members of the group. We refer to other factors as well – intelligence, motivation, dispositions of personality-structure – but we also refer to habits.

A habit is a learned response which persists over a considerable period of time without radical modification. The response exhibits a similar form and serves a similar function on repeated appearances – it is essentially 'the same' response each time. There are at least two classes of such habits: stimulus-response regularities which are elicited when certain conditions are present, and dispositions, which are tendencies towards a certain type of response, in appropriate stimulus-situations, but which vary over a range of performances. If we say that X picked up the evil habit of swearing while in the Navy, we imply that in a wide variety of circumstances (which could be specified incompletely) X is liable to use any one of a very wide range of verbal devices (which exactly we cannot predict for any given situation). Stimulus-response *bonds* are more restricted, precise, and predictable than dispositions. Both are probably the products of the most complex varieties of conditioning.

Much work has gone into the investigation of habits – how the strength of habits can be measured, how the strength of specific habits is determined, how some habits change and weaken, and how all habits form into hierarchies (some being more constantly evoked than others). It is not possible to summarize this work at present. The notion of habits simply serves as a rough indication of the more complex patterns or sequences of behaviour which are built up directly from such simple learning operations as conditioning (Pavlovian and instrumental). Having mentioned their existence, we can pass on to consider more complex and flexible learning procedures.

GENERALIZATION AND DISCRIMINATION

A conditioned response, when it is being established, shows a tendency to spread on both the stimulus and on the response sides. That is, in what is called stimulus generalization, the response tends to be elicited by any stimulus which is similar to the original stimulus. The closer the similarity the more readily is the response evoked. In response generalization a stimulus which has come to arouse a particular response may elicit a different response without special training.

This is not surprising, for after all, what is meant by a 'stimulus' or a 'response'? If the stimulus is the 'sound of a buzzer' or an 'electric shock', is this always precisely the same each time it occurs? There are small variations, such as length of time during which the sound occurs, the precise pitch or blend of tones which make the noise, etc., and, quite apart from the core of the stimulus situation, the buzzer always occurs in a context of sights, sounds, smells, bodily tensions which change considerably from one 'stimulus' situation to the next. Thus each time the buzzer sounds the stimulus situation is slightly different – the exact position of the subject, the perceptual field, the state of readiness, all change. It is only a similarity between one stimulus situation and the next which enables us to talk about the stimulus being repeated. Generalization of stimulus is implicit in simple conditioning. And response generalization is equally inherent – the animal's movements, which make the response, differ from one response situation to another. Even a simple movement – flexing a particular limb – differs from trial to trial in the force, speed, distance involved in the movement.

If this is thought to be overstating the case, how similar is each 'run' for a rat which runs through a maze twenty times, or the reflex of a boxer who leads a short left lead whenever an opponent presents a particular stance? However alike stimuli and responses may appear, they are never precisely alike on more than a few occasions. When we say that S_1 is the same stimulus as S_2, what we mean is that there is a very slight spread of effect, with a high degree of generalization.

Indeed the flexibility inherent in even the simplest responses which we call 'generalization' is vital for learning. If habits were strictly and rigidly bound to specific stimuli (namely, those which occurred in the situation in which they were originally formed), then there could be no further learning – no modification and adaptation of existing responses to new uses. It is only because any learned response can be generalized to other similar (in some respects) *and* at the same time different (in other respects) situations that adaptive behaviour is possible. A child not only avoids an article which gave it a burn, but all other objects which emit heat, glow, sizzle, and show the conventional signs of combustion-going-on. Again, a child which at one lesson has learned to toddle three or four steps can suddenly improve to ten or fifteen at the next lesson. Generalization of stimuli and responses is essential if learning is to take place. To give a maxim: generalization ensures similar responses in spite of differences between the stimuli; discrimination ensures different responses in spite of similarities between the stimuli.

Discrimination Learning. Generalization is a useful adaptive mechanism, but it must be subject to some kind of control, otherwise it might spread too far. Generalization ensures that successful responses spread and are modified to fit new situations, but there are also situations in which a given response will not fit at all. Thus over-generalized responses are not reinforced and behaviour is narrowed. This reverse or 'braking' process is called 'discrimination'. Clearly, the less R_1 generalizes away from S_1 towards S_2, $S_3...S_n$, the more accurate and precise is the discrimination between S_1 and other similar stimuli. Generalization expands and spreads learning operations: discrimination refines learning operations. Both are necessary controls.

Animals can learn to discriminate and act on the basis of their discriminations. In one experiment a rat is placed on a high stool (Lashley's 'Jumping Stand') which can be moved at various distances from a wooden or metal screen. The screen has two doors, close together, beyond which are two compartments. The doors have fixed to their surface movable coloured cards. The rat has to learn to select the door behind which food is regularly placed and to do this by discriminating between two distinct colours and the right-left alternative. The door leading to the food springs open easily as soon as the rat hits it in its leap – but the other door is locked so that if the rat selects it he bounces back and falls into a net, after which he is put back on the stool. The colours are varied between clear contrasts (black-white) and near colours (light-medium grey): the correct door (right-left) can also be varied in different sequences.

Again, monkeys have been presented with a choice between one or other of two food containers, each at the end of a long rope so that they can be hauled in towards the cage bars. The monkey can be given cues by varying the weight, size, and colour of the two containers – it has to learn to discriminate between similars (viz. between two near weights or between two near shades) in order to select the food container and leave alone the empty container. The variables which can be investigated in both these experiments are the number of errors made before learning is perfected, the length of the 'delay' interval between being placed at the choice point and the making of the choice response, the force with which the animal pulls or jumps, the rate at which learning develops

In these experiments the animal has to compare two separate – although similar – stimuli and select one or other as the clue for the 'correct' response. Other experiments make the animal compare successive stimuli and discriminate between them: in the 'Jumping Stand' experiment there is only one door and the animal has to learn that a light-grey card indicates 'food' and a dark-grey card indicates 'no food'.

The question which arises from the fact that animals can and do succeed in passing these discrimination learning tests is: 'How do they make discriminations?' 'How do specific cues come to elicit their responses?' In answer, C. L. Hull has put forward a theory which suggests that at the moment at which a reinforced response begins, ALL the stimuli acting on the receptive organs become associated with the response. Furthermore, particular stimulus-response association is strengthened every time that any part of the stimulus is present at the beginning of a successful response. Thus a stimulus-response association is developed in a continuous and cumulative manner – each particular S–R association being the cumulative product of all previous reinforcements (and non-reinforcements). If there are two possible responses to a given stimulus (right-door or left-door: light grey or dark grey), S–R sequence with the greater habit-strength will be forthcoming. Hull holds that the learning process is continuous from the very beginning of the first 'trial'. Making discriminations is a development of simple learning operations.

His view has been challenged by Krechevsky, who used the jumping-stand model as described above. Krechevsky noted two phases in the behaviour of rats during discrimination learning: the pre-solution explorations phase and the activities comprising an attempt at solution. The reactions of the rat during the pre-solution phase were not random but exhibited consistent patterns of response which Krechevsky calls 'hypotheses' or attempted solutions. All that training does during this phase, however, is to eliminate incorrect hypotheses. There is a sudden reversal of policy once the second phase begins. There is no such continuity or cumulative effect as Hull postulates.

This difference of theoretical interpretation is a familiar feature of learning theory. Psychology cannot yet offer tidy and empirically tested theories in this field. The examples are given to illustrate the kind of answer which is attempted when faced with the question: 'How do animals make discriminations?' Readers who wish to pursue the problem are referred to the list of recommended reading.

TRIAL AND ERROR LEARNING

It is within the discrimination-learning situation that vicarious trial and error learning emerges in a simple form. It has been noted that rats in the 'Reversed Cue' (Lashley Jumping Stand) experiments delay their response to a marked degree once the cues are changed. In the new pre-solution phase the animal is observed to hesitate, turning first towards one door and then towards the other; it does not jump confidently and quickly, but dithers. Once a new cue is introduced (a new colour-pair or a change in left or right choice) errors tend to be divided equally between the two alternatives for the first set of trials – as if the animal were trying out both before opting for one rather than the other. This kind of exploration and the shifting from one cue to the other while at the choice point is a form of trial and error which has already been described in the chapter on animal problem solving. Thus discrimination learning – a flexible operation – begins to merge into a familiar behaviour pattern of a more complex kind. It serves as an intermediate stage in the development of learning from simple conditioning to the more flexible trial and error activity.

Qualitative Discrimination and Social Habits. So far, we have confined the discussion to quantitative discrimination – simple sensory discrimination of colours, shapes, etc., in which some of the variables in both stimulus and response can be measured. In human subjects, however, there is a much more subtle qualitative discrimination learning in which generalized habits are refined. A good example is given by Professor C. E. Osgood.* A 2-year-old child learns to call his playmate 'friend'. Afterwards he learns to generalize this and call many other people 'friend', including some adult acquaintances of his parents. Later, he is taught 'manners' in the form of shaking hands with his playmates at parties. Without special training this social grace is extended to grown-ups, even to his father's casual visitors.

This is quite independent of any physical stimulus similarity relationship. There is nothing analogous to the recurring light-

* *Method and Theory in Experimental Psychology.* Oxford, 1953, p. 359.

grey patch on the left-hand door which is the cue for the rat's correct response. How then does such discrimination learning occur for the small child? Presumably the link is the concept of 'friend' – a class concept. This includes the child's own play-mates, is then extended to include the 'playmates' of the parents, and even adult associates of the family. Once the child learns to shake hands with one species of the genus 'friend' he extends the operation to other species. The notion of 'friend' (saying or thinking "This person is a "friend" ') is a mediating link. We have already noted, in discussing the development of conditioning, how a physical response (the eye-wink in Shipley's experiment, p. 114) acts as a mediating response. The concept of mediation as a crucial learning operation is one which is receiving considerable attention in experimental psychology. It appears to be one of the most useful mechanisms postulated so far.

THE MEDIATION HYPOTHESIS

Professor C. E. Osgood, of the University of Illinois, has made a most original contribution to the study of mediation and has developed a new theory of learning based upon an ingenious explanation of how mediation works. This theory is most readily accessible in his *Method and Theory in Experimental Psychology*, a book which may be compared with William James's *Principles of Psychology* in its thoroughness, vigour, and comprehensiveness; a land-mark in psychological literature. It is impossible to do justice to Osgood's theory – especially in his careful presentation of evidence – in a simple summary: the reader is, accordingly, referred to the original.* The point of this summary will be to show that the mediation process (which underlies generalization and discrimination) is basic to the learning of many higher skills.

Short-Circuiting of Responses. Whatever its explanation, 'short-circuiting' is a feature of all learned behaviour. For example, a rat is placed in a cage the floor of which is an electrifiable grill.

* Chapter 9, pp. 392–412.

A buzzer sounds and five seconds later the electricity is turned on. The rat leaps and twists in pain, clawing and dancing in an effort to escape from the painful stimulation. By accidentally turning a ratchet the current is switched off by the rat's random movements. After a series of repetitions the rat learns to turn the ratchet as soon as the buzzer sounds, thus preventing itself from receiving a shock. This 'foresight' cuts out all the intervening behaviour observable during the trial and error phase: it seems as if the reactions which only occurred at a late stage in the behaviour sequence are moved forward and now occur in anticipatory fashion. How does this shifting or short-circuiting take place?

C. L. Hull has made several attempts to explain the short-circuiting of instrumental learning which ends in a kind of anticipatory behaviour. The fact to be explained is that reactions originally elicited at one point in the behaviour sequence appear to move forward in the sequence and appear in an anticipatory manner. With these explanations we need not be concerned. Short-circuiting does occur and plays an important part in the formation of representational mediating responses.

Representational Mediating Responses. There are some acts the function of which is to serve as stimuli to yet further acts. These Hull calls 'Pure Stimulus Acts'. Such sequences are the basis of symbolic behaviour – being able to react in relation to the 'not here' and the 'not now' and to adjust to objects and events not present to perception at the time of acting. Osgood elaborates this notion of Hull's. He makes a distinction between:

(1) Those complexes of stimuli which elicit particular sequences of behaviour without any mediation. These are called 'stimulus objects'.

(2) Those complexes of stimuli which elicit mediation processes. These are called 'signs'.

A stimulus object, it should be noted, is not necessarily a concrete physical object or event, such as a tree or a flash of light or the feel of a tennis ball grasped in the hand. A sour taste in the mouth, getting an electric shock, a puff of wind on the face – these are all eligible as 'stimulus objects'.

Now, pure stimulus acts (acts which serve as stimuli to yet other acts) are set up by the process of short-circuiting, and serve as the basis for mediation. The explanation of their functioning for this purpose is as follows: Of the total behaviour elicited by a stimulus object, some parts are relatively 'tied' to the object; that is, such parts of the response sequence are dependent on the actual presence of the object for their occurrence. But other parts of the same response sequence are relatively 'detachable' from the stimulus object – they can occur independently of the presence of the object. For example, the animal swallows only when food is placed in the mouth and leaps about on the electrifiable grill only when the current is switched on. But the anxiety which occurs in the 'shock' situation can occur without the stimulus object (the shock) and the salivation can occur without food being presented. The former are 'tied' and the latter 'detachable' portions of the total response.

According to Osgood the short-circuiting is responsible for mediation. 'When other stimuli occur in conjunction with the stimulus-object, they tend to be conditioned to the total pattern of reactions elicited by the object: when later presented without support of the stimulus-object, these other stimuli elicit only the "detachable" reactions.'

At first the buzzer sound, or its fading reverberation, is present when the shock is given. Later the buzzer by itself evokes only *part* of the original response sequence which may become 'detached' – only the anxiety and agitation occurs. Any buzzer-like sound may then produce anxiety responses. The buzzer is now a sign of danger. An animal could be trained to take defensive-protective measures whenever a buzzer sounds. The stimulus is now a 'sign'. A wide range of stimuli can thus become associated with fragments of a behaviour sequence elicited by objects and so serve as signs of these objects.

A further consequence of this development of mediating reactions is that a mediating reaction evoked by a sign gives rise to

123

self-stimulation. Self-stimulation is a pattern of muscular and glandular reactions which, in human subjects, have distinctive conscious effects. These self-stimulations often serve as reinforcements to specific responses. For example, an animal stumbles across a sign of its natural prey – a smell, perhaps – and this is sufficient to set off a host of complex internal reactions which guide the overt activity known as 'hunting'. This is directed towards a non-perceived object indicated by the sign and the internal stimulations.

Instrumental Sequences. It is known that many living creatures start life with a number of inherited responses to certain forms of stimulation. It is on these innate responses that the complex repertoire of adaptive responses of the mature adult is built up. At first, relatively simple habits are formed through instrumental learning and conditioning operations. Later, somewhat disjointed series of isolated habits are integrated into a smoothly performed skill: the result of innumerable reinforcements and discriminations over a series of 'practices'.

The process which initiates the formation of skills or capacities would seem to be quite a simple one. Cues produced by preceding movements become conditioned to succeeding movements so that a link is formed and a continuous, integrated sequence results from the blending of what was formerly two disjointed sequences. In time, the initial stimulus sets off a long, smoothly executed automatic sequence, viz. 'running from A to B', 'turning left', 'discriminating a red disc shape from a red triangle shape'. Each of these is a simple skill. From the construction of one skill it is just one more stage to the fitting together of two or three or four skills to form a serial pattern (running a maze without taking any of the wrong turnings; turning downwards a lever within five seconds of a buzzer sounding, etc.).

The Function of Representational Mediation Processes. Certain stimulus-patterns, acting as signs, are always associated with SYSTEMS of mediating reactions. A buzzer may be a sign of an electric shock or the sign of food arriving: in each case there will be a different affective state-anxiety or food-anticipation feeling, which mediates appropriate response-sequences to the sign. Again the self-stimulation produced through the making of a specific mediating response is always associated with a system of skills. For instance, anxiety in a rat when it hears the buzzer may be associated with running, leaping, and clawing at a ratchet (in order to switch off the electricity).

Such systems as this are called 'Habit-family Hierarchies' by Hull. They have an important role in problem-solving behaviour. When placed in a problem situation the subject exhibits certain behaviour directed towards a specific goal. Thorndike's cats tried to escape from the puzzle box by squeezing through the bars: Köhler's apes tried to grab the food placed outside their cage with their hands. These were the most likely responses in view of the regularity with which they had been reinforced in the past. Once a specific response-sequence fails it is dropped and another emerges. In fact, behaviour will tend to become more random and varied the longer the problem remains unsolved. Which particular response emerges depends upon its position in the hierarchy, and this hierarchy is determined largely by biological factors. A monkey is more likely to solve a problem which requires the manipulation of a lever than a dog. The dog might use its paws or its teeth to pull the lever, but this response cannot have a high probability in the dog's habit-family hierarchy – while it has such a high-probability in the monkey's repertory of possible responses.

Hull divides hierarchies into two classes:

(1) Divergent Hierarchies, in which a stimulus situation S is associated with a number of alternative reactions R_1, R_2, R_3 ... R_n, and

(2) Convergent Hierarchies, in which a number of stimulus situations S_1, S_2 ... S_n are associated with one response R_x.

An example of a divergent hierarchy would be an 'anxiety' mediation process which might be associated with running, leaping, ratchet-turning in varying degrees, and an example of convergent hierarchy would be found in the fact that all distinctive stimuli along the course of the maze tend to become associated with the anticipatory goal-reaction – the mediating reaction in this case serving to bridge one skill sequence to another. Maier's experiment (Figure 3, page 41) on rats learning to fit separate sequences together in order to solve a maze-learning problem illustrated this process.

How Representational Mediation Processes Function. All this may seem rather abstract and unnecessarily technical, but it is un-avoidable in order to trace the complicated development of learning from the acquisition of simple habits to the formation of capacities and skills.

It may now be suggested that signs may be classified according to their power to evoke and sustain common mediating responses on the convergent hierarchy model (S_1, S_2, S_n being associated with one response R_x). If we use the symbol $\boxed{S}$ to denote a stimulus which functions as a sign – in order to differentiate it from the general class of mere stimuli – then we can proceed as follows. We can analyse the evocation of food-taking reactions by such different stimuli as the sight of the food-pail, the smell of the food, the recognition of the place where feeding usually takes place, by a diagram:

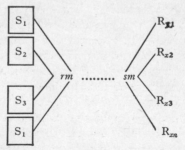

Figure 9

Here the signs S_1, S_2, S_3 ... each elicit a common mediating response *rm*; the self-stimulation resulting from this (*sm*) is conditioned to the initial reaction of several different instrumental sequences R_{x1} etc. Which sequence actually occurs depends on the particular conditioning history of the subject concerned. What happens here is that stimulus patterns associated with the same stimulus object become signs. How such signs develop and function will be described in detail in Chapter Nine. Smell or some other fragment of the former total situation becomes a sign of food and sets off some kind of food-oriented behaviour.

In order to make this point clear we might substitute the term 'significance' for the mediation process. We can then say that certain classes of signs (smells, shape of food containers, etc.) come to have the same significance for the animal. These signs, however different, mean the same thing to it, e.g. food. This is not to say that the animal is conscious of any meaning the sign may carry or has any experience analogous to the human reaction of sensing a particular smell and deducing 'bacon and eggs'. Nor does this imply that each animal which responds with food-anticipatory reactions to any given class of signs does so in exactly the same way as any other animal. This simplification attempts merely to bring out the way in which a convergent hierarchy of stimuli come to serve as signs for a particular kind of situation and hence are able to evoke a consistent response-sequence of an adaptive kind.

Likewise, when a rat hears the buzzer and responds to this as a sign of a coming shock it carries out a series of responses (running, jumping, clawing the ratchet, and turning it in a given direction); the object of all this is to prevent the shock. One might say that certain classes of instrumental skill-sequences (jumping, turning the ratchet, etc.) are associated with the same 'significance' (or even 'intention' in this case), namely to avoid pain. Again there is no implication that the rat has conscious grasp of the relationships involved in the way in which a human subject would through his ability to use language. The mentalistic talk is intended as a means of making the technical terminology a little easier to interpret.

Consider now a situation in which discrimination or choice

127

takes place; in which a human subject must select one or other of two instrumental sequences. Again the mediation hypothesis helps to suggest what happens.

$$S_1 - rm_1 - sm_1 \underset{rm_2 - sm_2}{\overset{}{\diagdown}} \begin{matrix} Rx_1 \\ \\ Rx_3 \end{matrix}$$
$$S_3 - rm_3 - sm_3$$

Figure 10*

With reference to Figure 10 Osgood illustrates this type of situation with the following concrete example. For a child the sight of playmate No. 1 on the other side of an open field (S_1) and simultaneously of playmate No. 2 on the other side of a stream (S_3) – each of these stimuli is associated with common mediating processes (rm_2 ... e.g. anticipation of play). But S_1 is associated with running in a straight line towards playmate No. 1 (instrumental sequence Rx_1), and S_3 is associated with searching, problem-solving behaviour evoked by the obstacle of the stream (Rx_3). A choice has to be made between the incompatible courses of action. So, if the child sees both its friends at once, which choice will be made? Rx_1 or Rx_3? The relative strengths of S_1-rm_1 and S_1-rm_2 as determined by prior learning decides which of two sequences is selected.

Finally, Osgood shows how the mediation process may function in long sequences of instrumental behaviour (Figure 11).

$$S_1 \underset{rm - sm}{\overset{rm_1 - sm_1}{\diagdown}} Rx_1 - S_2 \underset{rm - sm}{\overset{rm_2 - sm_2}{\diagdown}} Rx_2 - S_3 \underset{rm - sm}{\overset{rm_3 - sm_3}{\diagdown}} Rx_3$$

Figure 11*

A hunting animal hits upon some 'cold' spoor of its prey (S_1) which mediates rapid trailing responses (Rx_1). This behaviour

* Reproduced with permission from C. E. Osgood. *Method and Theory in Experimental Psychology*, Oxford, 1953.

brings it upon some warm spoor of its prey (S_2) which mediates quiet, stalking sequences (Rx_2). In turn this behaviour brings the animal to a clump of trees, the lower branches of which are trembling and crackling (S_3). At this stage the mediated self-stimulation is associated with gathering muscles preparatory to leaping (Rx_3). All these signs elicit anticipatory food-taking responses (*rm*) and the self-stimulation associated with these: it is this 'constant' or 'recurring' factor which gives 'purpose' to the sequence at each stage.

Organisms bring to each new and unfamiliar situation, as well as to familiar situations, one of two highly developed systems: (*a*) systems of mediating responses; (*b*) systems of instrumental sequences. Both are the product of previous learning.

New learning often requires modification in the mediating process elicited by the stimulus pattern (e.g. a buzzer may come to mean 'danger' instead of being a mere noise) and a modification in the instrumental sequence elicited by a specific mediator (e.g. the buzzer means 'danger' but running is not enough: the ratchet has to be turned).

It is the modification of well-established mediating processes and instrumental sequences which is the basis of adaptation. The way in which such modifications come about is complicated in the extreme; it involves the integration and interaction of many simpler learning operations of the kind discussed earlier in the chapter. It is one of the chief tasks of experimental psychology to discover exactly how this sort of development comes about, and so far only limited insight has been achieved. The very fact that hypothetical processes have to be postulated to which observable data have to be fitted indicates the tentative nature of all our present thinking in this field.

The Significance of the Mediation Hypothesis. Osgood's mediation hypothesis, which has been sketched here in barest outline, has many merits. It improves on the theories of Hull and Guthrie, two great pioneers in learning theory; it reconciles the conflict between behaviourism (reinforcement approach) and

Gestalt theory (perceptual reorganization approach). Above all, it enables a distinction to be made between previous learning and new learning which may be acquired in the task situation.

Thus the organism (whether rat or human) has a repertory of learned mediation processes. Many stimulus patterns come to have 'significance' so that what the organism perceives is organized in terms of specific mediators. Also there is a repertory of learned instrumental sequences associated with stimulus objects and with signs; hence characteristic approach-avoidance sequences, exploratory sequences, etc.

An adaptive response presents two aspects:

(1) The stimulus object elicits reactions. Other stimuli (signs) come to elicit parts of the original total response to the object under certain conditions (e.g. short-circuiting). From an investigation of these conditions it is possible to postulate the representational mediating responses at work in the given situation.

(2) From the observed behaviour mediated by these mediating responses it is possible to envisage a sequence in which the self-stimulations elicited by the mediators come to be conditioned to the initial responses of certain instrumental sequences – relating these to each other and to the stimulus factors.

The old learning which the organism brings to the situation is studied under (1), and the new learning established in the situation is studied under (2).

Thus mediation gives a suggestion of the way in which more complex learning begins to develop on the basis of simpler learning. We pass from single-stage stimulus-response learning to more complex learning operations, some of which can be met with in problem-solving behaviour.

For example, in the experiment in which rats are required to assemble separate pieces of training into one orderly sequence in order to solve the maze problem (described in Chapter Two, p. 32), mediation processes are required in any explanation of the results. All the separate stimuli which the rat receives as it runs the maze tend to become associated with the anticipatory goal-reaction of feeding – on the convergent hierarchy model. Without these mediating responses there could be no integration of the learned instrumental sequences needed to form the successful through run to the food box.

Again, in Maier's 'hat-rack' and 'pendulum' problems (described in Chapter Three) how do the subjects put together previously learned tricks in response to the new problem situation? Presumably the clues provided for the successful group set off mediating responses which elicit the proper set of instrumental sequences.

When we come in Chapter Nine to discuss language as a factor in thinking, the mediating process will be seen to be important in helping to explain how a stimulus comes to function as a sign. Some hint of this has already been given in this chapter, but it requires a more detailed treatment.

CONCLUSION

In this chapter a sketch has been drawn of the development of learning from simple learning operations to more complex ones of the kind found in problem-solving and concept formation. It might be objected that the complex types of human learning involved in thought cannot be adequately discussed in terms of simple learning operations and their immediate refinements. This must be admitted. There is still a gap to be bridged between the experimental data on conditioning, habits, and motor-skills and the more complex forms of learning practised by school-children and students. The higher forms of learning involve insight and purpose. There is some difference between a puppy being thrown into a pond and learning to swim and children taking swimming lessons and receiving instructions which are understood and followed. Nevertheless, such differences may well be matters of degree along a continuum. Sir Frederic Bartlett, who was Professor of Experimental Psychology at Cambridge between 1922 and 1952, has argued in a recent book that thinking is a high-level skill, requiring signs for its expression, yet exhibiting many of the characteristics of simpler bodily skills.*

It is true that the gap between the high-level skills which constitute thought processes and the simpler learning operations has not been bridged. Nevertheless some connexions can be discerned and certain analogies between insightful learning and simpler learning can be pointed out. This is why the Mediation Hypothesis model, however inadequate, has been used to tie together the loose ends and provide the basis for a discussion on the psychology of learning.

As Gilbert Ryle has said, thinking is largely a matter of 'drills and skills' – partly acquisition and partly performance of what has been acquired. The more we know about learning the more we are in a position to describe and explain thinking. Simple learning operations are among the necessary conditions of thought and complex skills are the essential, and sometimes the only, ingredients of thought.

Before leaving the subject of learning there is one more topic to consider; this is the transfer of training or the ways in which one habit or skill affects another. The following chapter will deal with this.

* Bartlett, Sir Frederic. *Thinking: An Experimental and Social Study.* London (Allen and Unwin), 1958.

SELECTED REFERENCES†

Bartlett, F. *Thinking: An Experimental and Social Study.* London (Allen and Unwin), 1958.

Bugelski, B. R. *The Psychology of Learning.* New York (Methuen and Holt), 1956.

Deese, J. *The Psychology of Learning.* New York (McGraw-Hill), 1952.

Hilgard, E. R., and Marquis, D. G. *Conditioning and Learning.* New York (Appleton-Century-Crofts), 1940.

Osgood, C. E. *Method and Theory in Experimental Psychology.* Chapters 8, 9 and 10. Oxford, 1953.

Woodworth, R. S., and Schlosberg, H. *Experimental Psychology.* Chapters 18, 19, 20, and 21. London (Methuen), 1955.

† See also p. 216.

CHAPTER SEVEN

Transfer and Interference

IN the previous chapter the basic learning operations, in so far as they are known to psychologists, were described and some indication given of their contribution towards the development of more complex functions such as thinking. Once a hierarchy of skills and capacities has been acquired, however, almost any new attainment must be built upon previous learning, and when two or more learning sequences interact in a situation the result may be one or other of three possibilities. They may have no effect on each other. On the other hand, something which is learned in one task may 'transfer' to another task in such a way that the latter is greatly facilitated. Finally, a first task may have an inhibitory or disturbing effect and interfere with the learning or application of the second one. Past learning often makes it easier to learn or practise new skills. A child who has mastered addition and subtraction finds it relatively easy to learn multiplication; a man who has been good at hockey and tennis in his youth may find it easier to become a good golfer in middle life than a man who takes up the game late in life but with no athletic past; a pianist may become a rapid and accurate typist with a minimum of practice. When previous learning improves or facilitates new learning this is called 'positive transfer'.

Sometimes, however, our previous learning makes it hard to acquire new skills or habits. It is not easy to recite the alphabet backwards as rapidly as we recite it from A to Z. An oboist trained on the simple-system instrument might have difficulty in getting used to a clarinet with its totally different fingering. When previous training has an adverse effect on new learning or adaptation, this is called 'negative transfer' or 'interference'. And, as has already been noted, there are neutral cases in which one skill appears to have no effect on another particular capacity.

It is not difficult to find examples of transfer effects. Habits learned with one hand can often be performed, without any training or practice, by the other hand. The German physiologist, Weber, reported that a surgeon of his acquaintance in teaching delicate surgical operations that sometimes had to be performed with the left hand and sometimes with the right, always trained right-handed students to perform the tricky operation with the left hand only: they could easily do the operation with the right hand without further training or practice. The skill transferred positively and automatically.

Transfer and interference between skills and habits is clearly a topic of importance not only in the study of learning but in considering all intelligent behaviour. All teachers need to know what kind of training is most likely to benefit the pupil when he is out on his own. The child in school has to meet situations which are very different from those which it deals with once it leaves school to take up work in an office or factory. Yet it is hoped that something of what the child learns at school will transfer to its later learning of a job and to its activities as a citizen. Also soldiers under training in the depot do not actually engage in live battles, but what they are taught is intended to make them capable of quickly adjusting to battle conditions in a way that would not be possible for a raw civilian. The singing teacher makes his pupils do all kinds of queer things which never are to be seen or heard on the concert platform or the operatic stage – yet without transfer effects of the studio exercises, no aria could be sung with control and artistry. Behind the skilled activity of every research scientist, surgeon, actor, or preacher, there is a long history of tedious and routine training without which the heights of expertness could never be attained. Transfer effects – positive and negative – although not easily tracked down are thus an important factor influencing our thought.

It is necessary to distinguish between two uses of the word 'transfer' in psychological literature. It sometimes means the transfer of a way of responding – a method, style, or pattern is carried over from one performance to another. In another sense 'transfer' means the effect of a primary task upon the learning or execution of the second task or performance. The first use describes a similarity in method between two separate performances: the second refers to the effect which this has in regard to the efficiency of the second performance.

There is also a different type of transfer situation. If a subject learns task A, then learns task B, and finally attempts task A again, the performance of A on the second occasion is sometimes improved and sometimes adversely affected by the intervening task. This phenomenon is called 'retroaction' – retroactive facilitation and retroactive interference.

Psychologists can produce many specimens of transfer, but they have no easy task in explaining them. What is being transferred from one situation to another? What mechanisms effect this transfer? What conditions determine when transfer will or will not occur? How does transfer operate in problem-solving, in concept attainment, in the use of signs in communication? We cannot stop to tackle all these interesting questions. A few illustrations will serve to indicate the significance of transfer as a factor influencing thinking operations.

EXPERIMENTAL DESIGN FOR TRANSFER

In studying transfer and retroaction the design used is similar to that used in the study of stimulus generalization in conditioning experiments.

The experimental group of subjects learns task A followed by task B (S_1–R_1 ; S_2–R_2). The control group rests from any specific activity and then learns task B (S_x–R_x; S_2–R_2). S_x–R_x indicates that the subjects are active in neutral ways during the 'rest' period. Positive transfer takes place if the experimental group learns task B more effectively than the control group.

Another design which studies retroaction follows the pattern:

Experimental Group: Learn A : Learn B : Test A
(S_1–R_1 : S_2–R_2 : S_1–R_1).
Control Group: Learn A : Rest : Test A
(S_1–R_1 : S_x–R_x : S_1–R_1).

Here positive transfer takes place if the re-test of A shows that the experimental group has improved more than the control group.

Transfer is estimated roughly in various ways. For example, if an experiment can be scored with reasonable accuracy so that subjects gain marks for success in learning the formula:

$$\frac{\left(\begin{array}{c}\text{Score of}\\\text{experimental group}\end{array}\right)\text{MINUS}\left(\begin{array}{c}\text{Score of}\\\text{control group}\end{array}\right)}{\left(\begin{array}{c}\text{Total possible}\\\text{score}\end{array}\right)\text{MINUS}\left(\begin{array}{c}\text{Score of}\\\text{control group}\end{array}\right)}\times 100$$

is used.

When the score for the experimental group equals that for the control group the transfer is zero. Any value by which the score of the experimental group exceeds that of the control group indicates a degree of positive transfer.

Into these experimental designs many tasks are fitted.

(1) Bilateral transfer from one hand to another or from one limb to another is used. For instance, a wooden cup is fitted with a long handle. From the cup is suspended a ball fixed to the inside of the cup by a length of strong cord. The task is to flip the ball into the cup while holding the handle with one hand only. All subjects are given 50 tries to test their skill. The experimental group then have 500 trials on the right hand while the control group rests. Both groups then have 50 trials on the left hand. In this experiment the experimental group showed over 60 per cent improvement on the original test, while the control group had only 28 per cent improvement. There has been a marked positive transfer of practice from the right to the left hand.

(2) Maze-learning tests provide another situation in which transfer occurs. Animal subjects can be set the task of learning to run mazes, while humans can be blindfolded and made to learn a maze by tracing the pathways with the fingers. The experimental group learns maze 'A'; the control group rests. Both groups then learn maze 'B'. In such experiments, the experimental group learns the second maze much more quickly and

much more effectively than does the control group. Practice in maze learning transfers from one maze problem to another. Familiarity, not surprisingly, is a marked advantage.

(3) In the field of problem-solving transfer is an ever-present factor. In most problem-solving experiments it is not taken into account simply because of the difficulty in finding out what the past training of the subject has been. Negative transfer is quite clearly an important factor within the problem situation – false leads and beginning a task with an activity which has inhibiting effects on the emergence of the very operations required for the successful solution of the problem may prove fatal to a successful solution.

It was noticeable in Ruger's experiments using mechanical puzzles that subjects coming to a specific puzzle for the first time did much better than a group who had been successful in solving a puzzle which had misleading similarities with the new puzzle: negative transfer operated to the disadvantage of the group with previous experience.

On the other hand, Thorndike noticed in his puzzle-box 'escape-problem' experiments with cats that a cat which had learned to escape by manipulating one kind of escape mechanism would more quickly learn a quite different type of mechanism than an unpractised cat. This skill appeared to transfer positively even when an adaptation was required.

Quite clearly when a problem is tackled previous training influences the performance: the subject is either suitably trained to deal with the situation or his prior bias in learning ill-qualifies him for the task in hand. At the common-sense level we all know the type of learned scholar who is helpless at practical jobs of even the simplest kind and of the able 'practical' man who cannot understand elementary theory – in statistics or law for example. How precisely positive and negative transfer effects build up and operate in individual cases is not known: we only know that such effects operate to assist or hinder the efforts of the problem-solver.

Almost any human capacity or function transfers – perceptual discriminations, motor skills, grasp of abstract principles or methods, emotional attitudes, 'set'. Although much work has been done on transfer as a phenomenon, its precise working has yet to be investigated in detail. What do we know, in general, about transfer?

TRANSFER AS GENERALIZATION OF RESPONSE

Using the experimental design for producing stimulus generalization in conditioning studies, it is possible to study the situation in which the response is kept constant but the stimulus varied in the two tasks:

> Experimental group: Learn S_1–R_1 Learn S_2–R_1
> Control group: Rest   Learn S_2–R_1

In this experiment the response is generalized to stimuli not present in the original conditioning. The upshot of many experiments of this design is to show that the more similar is the stimulus S_1 to the stimulus S_2, the more successful is the learning of the new task. If the difference between S_1 and S_2 is increased the learning becomes less efficacious. Positive transfer seems to be a function of similarity between stimuli, in this type of situation.

Another experiment keeps the stimuli constant but varies the response:

> Experimental group: Learn S–R_1 Learn S–R_2
> Control group: Rest   Learn S–R_2

Under most conditions the new response R_2 is incompatible with R_1 and negative transfer results; this result, however, is not altogether consistent.

The general conclusions about transfer phenomena appear to be generally agreed upon:

(1) Whether positive or negative transfer results depends primarily upon the character of the data to be learned or practised.

(2) The most significant factor is the degree of similarity involved in the stimulus-response situation; that is, the relation of similarity between S and R determines the probability of positive or negative transfer effects. How does this turn out in actual cases? The principles involved are relatively simple.

(1) Similarity between stimuli coupled with similarity between responses generally leads to positive transfer.

$$S_1-R_1 \quad : \quad S_1-R_1 \qquad \text{(positive)}.$$

(2) Similarity between stimuli coupled with differences between responses generally results in negative transfer.

$$S_1-R_1 \quad : \quad S_1-R_2 \qquad \text{(negative)}.$$

In (1) the second task is merely repeating or practising the first task and maximum positive transfer results. As the differences in similarity increase, the positive transfer weakens. In (2) the stimuli are similar but the response is different in the two tasks. This is well illustrated by a conditioning experiment in which a dog was trained to respond differently towards a circle and an ellipse. Food was presented immediately after the circle and an electric shock accompanied the ellipse. The ellipse was slowly changed until it approached the point at which the difference between the circle and ellipse could no longer be easily discriminated. At this stage the dog exhibited something like a 'breakdown'. It could no longer cope with the situation and produce two radically different responses 'Prepare to eat'; 'Prepare for pain'. The two stimuli were too similar to signal the difference: circle–food: ellipse–shock. There must be a clearly discernible difference between stimuli for them to act as signals or distinct responses.

Between (1) and (2) lie a wide range of variations. If there is some degree of similarity between responses in two different tasks, there will be a corresponding degree of positive transfer. As the similarity between responses R_1 and R_2 decreases, the amount of positive transfer possible diminishes. As soon as a clear-cut dissimilarity or incompatibility between the responses appears, negative transfer begins, and this gets worse with increasing 'clashes' between the character of the responses involved in the two tasks.

This kind of transfer is clearly founded on stimulus generalization as its basic mechanism. Obviously there are much more complicated types of transfer than this. We have selected the simple case in order to indicate how transfer effects are a development of more simple learning operations.

RETROACTION

A further basic phenomenon in this field is retroactive facilitation or interference. This is closely related to recall and recognition – the linking up of a present situation with past learning and past perceptions.

As will be remembered, the experimental design for testing the effects of an intervening activity between learning and recall or reproduction is:

Experimental group:	Learn A	Learn B	Recall A
Control group:	Learn A	Rest	Recall A.

Either the experimental group exhibits facilitation or interference of recall because of task B or there is no effect from B at all. In the latter case the experimental group and the control group do not show any differences in their recall capacity.

Again there is a further experimental set-up which investigates what is called 'proactive' interference or proactive facilitation as the case may be:

Experimental group:	Learn B	Learn A	Recall A
Control group:	Rest	Learn A	Recall A.

From a large number of experiments, in which the conditions within the general design have been varied, several general conclusions have been drawn about retroactive and proactive effects.

(1) Many of the humdrum activities of everyday life have an inhibitory effect on the retention and recall of former learning. There have been experiments in which the control group have

learned a skill and then been made to recall what they have learned after a period of sleep. The experimental group, who learned the same task, proceed with normal working activities while the control group is sleeping. The experimental group show marked deterioration in the recall of the prior learning. Fatigue through activity accounts for only a little of this, since tests given to the group before recall show them to be reasonably alert and unimpaired in their readiness to cope with some further tasks.

(2) To a certain limited extent inhibition or deterioration in recall increases with the amount of interpolated activity. This factor, however, is not nearly so influential as the character of the interpolated activity.

(3) The key factor is the kind of learning material involved in the tasks. Certain methods, strategies, activities fit better together in sequences of the kind A–B–A or B–A–A than others.

LEARNING SETS

H. F. Harlow of Wisconsin University has postulated the acquisition of what he calls 'learning sets' as one of the intermediary stages between simple conditioning and the more complex use of learning in problem-solving behaviour. Learning sets are possibly the mechanism which makes transfer of the positive type possible.

Harlow argues that the behaviour of human beings is not to be understood in terms of the results of single, isolated learning situations, but rather in terms of the changes which are effected through multiple (though comparable) learning tasks. The most important learning is the formation of learning sets – learning how to learn, how to move from trial and error to insight or rationality, and hence to the control of a problem situation.

The way in which such learning sets are formed was studied by Harlow in an experiment in which both children and monkeys were used as subjects.

The subject is placed before an apparatus. The apparatus consists of a grill through which the subject can reach and select only one or other of two distinctive objects, e.g. a yellow ball or a square blue box. Each object covers a well in which a delectable reward can be placed – but the reward is placed in one or other of the wells.

The subject has simply to learn which of the objects is the clue to the hidden reward. The particular pairs of objects are changed throughout the experiment and the right or left position for the correct choice is varied. In all 344 problems using many different pairs of stimuli can be set in Harlow's experiment.

In the case of all the subjects there had been no previous laboratory learning; the entire discriminatory learning set for each subject could thus be studied throughout its entire development. What the subjects were required to do was to learn how to learn. They began with easy problems and progressed to more difficult ones. They had to transfer what had been learned in one problem to the task which faced them in the next. Each subject was given a fixed number of attempts at each task before moving on to the next.

The results of this experiment were striking.

For example, the score of correct responses on the second attempt at each new task is given in the table:

No. of Tasks Attempted	% of Correct Responses
In early tasks 50%	of correct responses
25	70
100	80
200	88
300	95

The first attempt at a new task showed a change in effectiveness as the experiment progressed. In the first eight discriminations the monkeys at their second attempt at each problem did little better than 3 per cent above chance in selecting the correct clue. But in the last fifty-six discriminations their performance fell only 3 per cent below perfection.

It was discovered that, after the formation of a learning set, a single attempt, if correct, often constituted the solution of the problem. The subject had grasped the principle to be followed.

In the final phase of the experiment Harlow's monkeys could solve between twenty and thirty consecutive problems without error, following only one trial on each separate problem in which the correct solution happened to emerge. As Harlow says, 'The learning set is a mechanism that changes the problem from an intellectual tribulation to an intellectual triviality.' Whatever tricks were played on the monkeys by varying the order of cues, reversing cues and rendering the problem increasingly complex, they always managed to adapt themselves and at greater speed as the series of problems proceeded. What the monkey acquired was not an increasing number of habits or associations but a generalized ability to learn *any* discrimination problem. Difficulty and complexity did not matter – the subject could easily attack a problem of increased difficulty because of the strengthened 'set' for this type of problem.

Harlow points out that the monkeys which were wild and intractable at the beginning of the experiment were tame and co-operative at the end of it. A social learning set had been built up. Each contact with a human experimenter had constituted a learning task and each experimenter had represented a 'problem'. Learning to react cooperatively to one or two experimenters was followed by greater adaptation towards the next human being with whom the monkey had to deal. As a by-product the monkeys had been trained to become good experimental subjects.

The formation of learning sets – often of extreme complexity – is probably the most important single factor in eliminating errors and allowing positive transfer effects to build up within the problem situation. Adaptation becomes flexible and discriminating at the same time, a fine balance is automatically maintained between generalization and discrimination. The transfer of past learning to new situations – smoothly, unconsciously, and yet appropriately and systematically – comes about through such mechanisms as that of the learning set. How exactly such mechanisms originate and develop and blend with each other into a balanced repertory of available skills and capacities we do not know. The broad outlines of the process are all that present-day psychology can indicate.

TRANSFER AND THINKING

Not many experiments have been carried out in which transfer effects have been studied as factors determining the course of thought processes. Even in studies of problem-solving or concept attainment the transfer effect emerges as a by-product and is not the main topic of interest for the experimenter.

What seems to follow from transfer-retroaction studies is that interference transfers automatically from one situation to another and that there is little that one can do about it. Positive transfer can be promoted if appropriate mediating factors are introduced to link prior learning to present task-requirements. This is shown in Maier's 'Hat-rack' and 'Pendulum' problems (Chapter Three, pp. 56-8). In these experiments intelligent subjects who understood the problem and were given the simple materials required to solve it failed to do so if they were without previous practice and useful directions or hints. Other subjects with previous training on parts of the solution only went forward to a successful solution if they were provided with visual cues or verbal instructions which reminded them of the principles or strategies involved. Only if this mediating factor was present did positive transfer take place and the previous training merge into the practical tackling of the problem. The thinker must get this mediating factor either by providing it himself by defining the principle or method involved or by being provided with it from an external source – a visual cue, a written or spoken direction or hint from somebody else or from books.

The conclusion for the study of thinking would therefore appear to be:

Positive transfer of relevant past training to a present task only takes place if the subject can make use of a mediating factor: this may come from cues within the task situation or as a result of the activity of the thinker.

Negative transfer will occur if the wrong sort of activity is introduced. The thinker must eliminate activities which have negative transfer effects at the start and must be provided with appropriate mediation processes for linking past learning with the specific task requirements of the present problem. Transfer-retroaction studies are simply the investigation of the conditions under which past experience succeeds or fails to be appropriately applied to the needs of the present. How does the appropriate kind of mediation process come about in this situation or in that? This would seem to be the crucial question in attempting to understand the relevance of studies of transfer retroaction in relation to thinking.

CONCLUSIONS: LEARNING AND THOUGHT

Transfer as a factor involved in the capacity to learn and apply what one has learned is thus an important condition of thought. Much thinking is very largely the acquisition of new learning or the application of old learning to a situation – although it is never merely learning, it is also the attempt to satisfy a need and the striving to express some facet of the personality.

Learning is often the most obvious factor involved in thought. For example, when a student works over a proof or argument which he has already followed in a lecture, he is thinking. Or when a person who has already mastered French and Latin decides to buy a book in order to teach himself Italian he is going to adapt his previous skills in acquiring foreign languages to a new case. Even the brilliant innovator – the composer of a highly original symphony which exhibits striking new harmonies or tricks of orchestration – cannot begin to work without a conventional training in his craft. Even creativity involves learning and transfer.

'Learning', in brief, is a term which has a broad and a narrow meaning. In its narrow sense it refers to specific operations such as conditioning, stimulus generalization, discrimination, mediation, and so forth. In its broader implications it covers all modifications or changes in behaviour in which the effects of previous training are operative. As D. M. Johnson has suggested, there is a scale of development along which adaptive behaviour ranges from simple conditioning at one end to problem-solving at the other. One sort of learning grows and blends with every other until highly complex hierarchies of habits, skills, dispositions, and ineptitudes form a system which determines the obvious pattern of behaviour exhibited by the subject. Learning is both a determining condition and a recurring content of thought processes.

Even so, learning is not the only factor involved in thinking, however dominating a role it may play. As Ryle has reminded us, when we describe a person as 'thinking' we do not refer to a simply definable activity like 'running' or 'digesting food'. Thinking may involve many or few of several quite distinct sorts of activity: there are many different things which a thinker can be up to.

And just as there are many different tasks any of which qualify as being classified as 'thinking', so the variables which determine the origin and progress of these activities are various and complex. Learning is certainly among these variables; perhaps it is the most influential in shaping the character of the processes and their products. But there are other variables involved – motivation of the thinker, motor skills, perceptions, personality structure (intelligence, receptivity, rigidities, etc.), and social conditioning.

At present no treatment of these variables – either separately or taken together – can give anything other than a very incomplete account of what makes us think in the ways that we do. And no branch of psychology is more limited and tentative than learning theory. Psychologists have only tackled problems in this field since the period beginning with the close of the First World War (since 1919). In this and in the previous chapter a sketchy account has been given of some of the ways in which the psychology of learning is relevant to the study of thought. It may be enough to show how it is impossible to study human behaviour too abstractly. It is only as a matter of convenience that we isolate a particular function such as 'thought' for separate study: but human beings are not machines which switch over from one particular activity to another: everything they do fits into a complex system which is a totality, and when one discusses one particular psychological function it is inevitable that one is led to consider a number of others from which the focused function cannot be disconnected.

The next line of attack upon the conditions of thought is to study it from the point of view of its motivation. What is it which evokes, guides, and directs a thought process from start to finish, giving it a goal and consistency in working towards it? This question is the one to be discussed in the following chapter.

SELECTED REFERENCES

Deese, J. *The Psychology of Learning*. New York and London (McGraw-Hill), 1952.

Harlow, H. F. 'The Formation of Learning Sets.' *Psychological Review*, 1949.

Johnson, D. M. *The Psychology of Thought and Judgment*. Chapter 5. New York (Harper), 1955.

Kingsley, H. L. *The Nature and Conditions of Learning*. New York (Prentice Hall), 1946.

Vinacke, W. E. *The Psychology of Thinking*. Chapter 8. New York and London (McGraw-Hill), 1952.

Woodworth, R. S., and Schlosberg, H. *Experimental Psychology*. Chapters 18 to 21. London (Methuen), 1955.

CHAPTER EIGHT

The Dynamics of Thinking: Motivation and Thought

THINKING is a complex activity. In the case of problem-solving, thought begins when a problem is recognized by the agent, proceeding through various stages until either a solution is attained or the attempt to find one is abandoned.

Such activity demands concentration and effort as well as skill and intelligence. The psychologist is faced, therefore, with the task of explaining how it is that any particular thought process keeps on the move and how it is organized through what may be a series of distinct phases from the beginning to the end of the problem. What factors help to organize our thinking in a specific direction? How do we keep to the point and exclude irrelevant interests?

This question takes us into the largely uncharted field of the motivation of conduct. Most of the theories available are speculative and any answer to the question, 'What factors assist in directing behaviour in this or that direction?' is bound to be tentative; a matter of opinion rather than knowledge. Nevertheless a general answer to the question, 'What keeps us thinking about an unsolved problem?' must be attempted.

It is a familiar fact that the performance of a person, whether in sport or intellectual pursuits, does not always exhibit his ability. We can discover, over a series of trials, what X's average is and what is the level of his best performance. But sometimes he falls a long way below his average. Why do such lapses occur? Sometimes fatigue, physical ailment, or other such factors account for the failure. But on other occasions it is X's motivation which is wrong. Either he is under-motivated and cannot apply his skill purposefully to the task or else he is over-motivated and is so anxious to succeed that somehow he loses control of his energies and skills. Ability and sound training are not sufficient by themselves to guarantee success. The agent must be properly motivated also.

Again, we often start wondering what a person's motives were only when the unexpected and surprising has happened; when a brilliant student suddenly gives up his studies and goes to sea or a politican leaves one party and joins another. What has happened to bring about this result? What was the agent up to? What was his motive?

However, we can also ask about the motivation of ordinary, expected behaviour. The word 'motivation' is probably misleading in such contexts. Just what is 'motivated' behaviour? All we want to know when we inquire into a person's motivation are certain facts about his situation. We want to know (*a*) what specific objective or goal was attained as a result of his performance; or what objective he failed to attain; (*b*) what means were appropriate to achieve the goal; (*c*) what information was at the agent's disposal.

Motivated behaviour is simply goal-directed behaviour. We want to know what X was trying to achieve in doing what he did and, further, what was the reason or the urge or the need or aversion behind his overt activities. It is this factor of what is 'behind' the goal-directed behaviour which has caused most difficulty for psychologists.

Most psychologists have tended to think of a goal-directed behaviour sequence in three stages. First, they postulate that the agent experiences a particular state of inner disturbance; he is in a state of tension, unrest, or disequilibrium which must be brought to quiescence. Secondly, he is in this condition in virtue of a particular stimulus impinging upon him from his physical and social environment; this is either a perception directed towards a goal object or a sign pointing towards the existence of a goal situation yet to be realized. The goal may be the attainment of some physical object, the achievement of social recognition, or the solution of a problem. Finally, through a series of actions the agent either attains the goal situation, and in so doing terminates his condition of unrest, or fails to do so, and withdraws from the environmental situation which imposed this complex activity upon him. Thus it has been said that in goal-directed behaviour, bodily energy is mobilized and selectively directed towards parts of the environment. Outwardly the behaviour of the agent is directed towards a specific goal; this sequence is initiated and sustained by an inner state in which energy is released and organized in a highly specific manner. The 'motive' is no longer located in a behaviour pattern but in this special inner condition of the agent.

This approach is basic to several theories of motivation, although cogent objections may be raised against it. For example, consider the 'biological survival theory' of goal-directed behaviour.

This particular theory regards such behaviour as having its origins in certain fundamental biological needs, such as those for food, water, a mate, or shelter. These primary needs, which must be satisfied if the agent is to survive, become the basis for the development of secondary or derivative needs.

For example, a chimpanzee can learn to obtain its food from a slot machine by inserting coloured poker chips. The chimpanzee next learns to obtain the poker chips from a second machine worked by a different mechanism.

After a time the acquisition of the chips becomes a goal in its own right. Even when not activated by hunger, the chimpanzee will solve various obstruction-test problems in order to win chips which it proceeds to hoard. Moreover, it will learn to select chips of that colour which has a higher value in terms of the amount of food it will procure. The chimpanzee has learned the need to accumulate a kind of money, but this has grown out of the more basic organic need for food. In an analogous manner, although the process is much more complicated, all our complex human wants and desires and hankerings are alleged to derive from basic organic drives; such as drives which must be satisfied if we are to survive.

Against this theory there are several objections. In the first place the hypothesis that all goal-directed behaviour must be preceded by a state called a 'drive' (or biological need), even if this is secondary and derivative, is difficult to test, and is, in any case, improbable.

There appear to be many instances of goal-directed activity in which a vigorous need, drive, or tension is notably absent. Medical science can even produce many examples in which vital organic needs do not produce any directed behaviour in the way in which hunger and sex drives do. Vitamin B_{12} is necessary for life; without it a human being will die of pernicious anaemia. Yet a person suffering from vitamin B_{12} deficiency does not behave in a goal-directed manner, seeking out or craving for substances containing the vitamin. Apart from this sort of criticism it is difficult to see how tissue or organic needs could be the basis for the growth of complex secondary needs since in a highly organized modern society individuals are well cared for and protected from birth so effectively that they rarely experience any vigorous organic need for food, warmth, or security.

Of course it is argued by the biological survival theorists that all basic needs are formed in early infancy when primary needs for food, drink, security, etc. are dominant and powerful. Thus the first experiences of life determine and mould a system of innate needs and form the basis for all future motivational states. Adult motivational conditions are conditioned, reinforced, or sublimated versions of what were originally organic drives – feeble now, or non-existent, but once vigorous and dominant in the first year or so of life. This is the standpoint of Freud. He holds that motives of all kinds have their origin in the 'Id', which is a complex set of dispositions which constitute the residual, primitive 'animal' impulses in human nature and are the source of all psychological energy. C. L. Hull has a similar view; he holds that an agent only responds to objects and situations which have been associated with the reduction of primary drives in the past and only if the secondary drives thus associated with primary needs have been complexly reinforced.

Motives are a species of habit being tripped off by appropriate stimuli.

It may be the case that primitive, or organic, drives, activated vigorously in infancy, form the source of all goal-directed behaviour on the basis of a structure formed in early life. This hypothesis cannot, however, be tested by empirical methods and there are considerations against it. For one thing the study of human and animal learning has shown how flexible and capable of refinement behaviour is. New skills and habits can be acquired at most periods of life. It would be odd if goal-directed behaviour were the product of a fixed and rigid system of dispositions formed in the first two years of life. If we can go on developing our system of skills and habits why not our motivational states as well? However, the notion of a 'motivational state' is itself suspect. Each type of goal-directed behaviour is given a highly specific initiating condition (tension, disequilibrium, etc.) which determines the overt activity. This looks like a revival of the discredited faculty-psychology, which explains nothing (viz. X displays angry behaviour because of a condition of rage within him).

Nevertheless it is plausible to suggest that variations in behaviour directed towards a specific goal are functionally dependent upon antecedent conditions of some kind or another. Sometimes a vigorous drive may be included in such antecedent conditions. At other times the agent may be in relation to factors in his environment in such a way that we may describe him as having a need or want or urge. Such needs are defined in terms of the past learning of the agent, his present situation and his information concerning certain parts of his environment. Once the needs have been defined they may enter into the antecedent conditions which partly determine the goal-directed behaviour. Thus when considering the motivation of a person from the viewpoint of psychology we are concerned with certain crucial factors.

(1) We want to discover relevant antecedent conditions which initiate the behaviour.

(2) We want to know what specific perceptual and motor sets are initiated by these conditions.

(3) We want to know which specific goal is selected and fixated by the agent in this process.

(4) We want to describe the activities of the agent in reaching or failing to reach the goal.

This pattern of activity, from start to finish, will be highly idiosyncratic depending on the personality of the agent, his particular history and capacities, as well as upon the context of action. Yet in spite of the individual differences between one goal-directed sequence and another there is much to be said for Freud's view that there are certain objectives which *all* men must seek. Whatever the particular physical and social environment, and however circumstances may vary, there are typical kinds of goal which are common to all men and which arouse behaviour directed towards them. A wide variety of human activity is determined by similar motives. Moreover, not all such basic patterns of activity and the conditions under which they occur are capable of being easily discriminated either by the agent or by observers. There are 'unconscious' factors which are crucial in the description and explanation of goal-directed behaviour. Hence the need for psychologists to ask of ordinary and unexceptional actions, 'Why did X do that?' Philosophers may object that it is odd to ask such questions as 'What led X to do such and such' of such activities as choosing a wife or a career, taking up tennis at the age of 40, or smoking a pipe. Apart from conventional explanations of such normal behaviour, which are valid as far as they go, there is some force in the kind of interpretations of deliberate actions offered by psycho-analysts of the Freudian and other schools.

In trying to suggest how thought processes are initiated and sustained it is as well to concentrate on the problem of describing the relationship between the goal-directed behaviour pattern and its antecedent conditions. By selecting a modified and non-controversial standpoint derived from psycho-analysis and its derivatives we can do this in a manner which is sufficient for our purposes. No claim is made on behalf of what follows as a theory. It is intended merely as a descriptive model for relating goal-directed behaviour patterns to their antecedent conditions.

DYNAMIC PSYCHOLOGY AND MOTIVATION

Psycho-analysts and clinical psychologists whose business it is to diagnose and treat the various types of neurosis and psychosis have often developed, in the course of their thinking, a general theory of motivation. Although divided amongst themselves into various rival 'schools' and inclined to drift rather far from firm empirical moorings, there is much to be gained from an eclectic approach to this source. A. H. Maslow* presents an admirable synthesis of material from psycho-therapy reinforced by data from other fields of psychology. Maslow makes some common-sensical points about goal-directed behaviour which are refreshing. He points out that it is the whole person who is motivated and not just some part of him. Every psychological function is changed in motivated activity – perceptual set, memories, emotions, thought processes are all reorganized in terms of the logic of the situation.

Furthermore, basic needs are analysable at different levels. To take an example. If a man's activities all seem to be directed towards the acquisition and hoarding of money we might ask 'Why?' He may want to buy a particular house or a specific automobile or to invest the money over a long period. This desire is, in a sense, his reason for saving. But why does he do this or that with the money once he has got enough of it? Is it to bolster up his self-esteem and win the social approval of certain other people? Here is a deeper kind of 'motive' for his activity. Does he feel, in an obscure way, that only people who are socially powerful are capable of getting respect and affection? And is this attitude the result of some peculiar maladjustment that gives rise to such needs as 'love-through-dominance'? Ultimately it

* Maslow, A. H. *Motivation and Personality*. New York (Harper), 1954.

may be that surface needs, like the need for money to buy a car and a big house, can be traced to one or other of a number of more basic needs. And these basic needs may be common to most men in different cultures and at different periods of history. Most societies may provide outlets for the satisfaction of the need for self-respect and the approval of other people – although in widely differing forms. And a specific behaviour-pattern may satisfy not merely one but several needs at the same time. Needs may have to be traced not only in depth but along several dimensions before the action they determine has been explained. For example, the acquisition of a mate satisfies not only the sex drive but also needs for security, affection, leadership, or dominance; and the satisfaction of a particular need may require the prior satisfaction of several more basic needs.

Therefore one would expect to find many social needs – some 'basic' and common to most men in most societies, others dependent upon local conditions; a powerful clique, a historical situation, a prolonged crisis. Are there any recurrent social needs which might influence thinking?

In most societies people want a good opinion of themselves both in their own eyes and in those of others. Self-respect and popular esteem are active needs. If a man is deprived of them he becomes anxious, tense, and restless. Whether to satisfy a sense of mastery or achievement or to stand well in the estimation of others, a piece of thinking may well be influenced by this sort of need. Abilities are rarely useless, and to be able to exercise one's wits may be a means to self-respect and general esteem.

Again, most people have some capacity or skill which has been developed to a degree of competence. It soon becomes necessary for anyone conscious of such a capacity to exercise it. Otherwise frustrations results. If a problem or difficulty gives opportunity for the exercise of talent then a person with the skill will have an urge to exercise it simply as a means of self-expression and self-gratification.

Again curiosity seems to be deep-seated in many living creatures. Monkeys, without either reward or punishment, will wrestle with mechanical puzzles and rats will endure an electric shock in order to explore some unfamiliar section of their pro-blem-cage. Problems, puzzles, difficulties of all kinds appear to have an intrinsic fascination for most people. Children do not need to be stimulated into curiosity and into seeking answers to difficult questions. The desire to obtain knowledge and insight, to explain what is unfamiliar, to find out how things work, to acquire new skills, is a strong one: perhaps it is based on a basic need for security, for an orderly, clear-cut, controlled world-environment?

Again the tackling and solving of a problem brings about a definite and intensely pleasurable affective state, while the wrestling with conquerable difficulties produces just that degree of discrepancy between affective level and perception that pro-duces pleasure rather than pain. This experience in itself might be part of the goal for the thinker – itself a motive for thought.

Finally, most pieces of successful thinking receive some kind of social reinforcement. The education of most middle-class boys and girls in Britain has long been a treadmill of scholar-ships, prizes, graded class-lists, honours, and medals. The praises and admonitions of parents and schoolmasters begin very early in life. Thus ego-needs (self-respect), social needs (praise, achievement), as well as security (winning a good job through education), all combine to make many intellectual tasks strongly motivated. Competition, too, enters into social training from its earliest days.

Thus to develop and exercise intelligence is an activity which has its own characteristic goals. These are quite distinguishable from other goals which might enter into a thought process. Almost any need might influence a thinker in addition to intrin-sically intellectual ones: e.g. attachment needs (the desire to justify oneself before friends and benefactors), security needs, ego-needs, social needs. In some cases thinking might be the only way to end a painful state of boredom and inactivity. If one is trapped in a railway carriage in a fog some puzzle in chess or bridge might enable one to endure the confinement. And is it accidental that many great philosophers have been gentlemen with lots of leisure? Even a soldiering philosopher like Descartes had to take to metaphysics when snowed up in a remote village during a winter campaign.

THE MOTIVATION OF THOUGHT

We do not know very much about motivation. It is a complex condition into which psycho-therapy has given us some insight, but not enough upon which to build a sound general theory.

There is little difficulty in finding adequate motives for any bit of reflection or thought. Indeed without adequate motivation nobody would ever begin to think vigorously or having begun would persist until the end of a difficult problem. Although motivation is an essential factor in determining the character of thought, what specific motives operate in initiating and guiding any given thought process depends upon the context. The same problem may be tackled and solved by X and Y from entirely different needs. For example, one man may become a great mountaineer because he wants to exercise a body weakened by a serious illness in childhood; another man may achieve competence in the same field because of the glory he gets from his activities; another may achieve analogous success because it ties up with his passion for botany and geology and geography. Another may do it for sport, and yet another to prove to himself that he is tough and self-reliant. One could extend this list for a long way – and also show that it is rare for only one need to be satisfied in a particular activity. Also it is evident that that one particular need can find an outlet in several quite different activities.

Motivation is thus an essential factor in thinking. But it is not always directly connected with the form and content of the products of thinking. A thought process and its results might be similar under very different conditions of motivation – assuming, of course, a non-pathological situation or one in which neurotic mechanisms do not necessarily operate (e.g. solving a mathematical problem).

SETS AND ATTITUDES

Not all behaviour is determined by basic needs: not all behaviour is motivated. Some responses or series of responses are tripped off by isolated stimuli and are the product of conditioning or complex habit hierarchies or even instinct or other innate response-patterns.

One group of mechanisms which operates during thinking and functions as an organizing, controlling, and directive influence is that referred to by the term 'set'. The term 'set' as used by psychologists is ambiguous. J. J. Gibson has analysed the term into at least eight distinct meanings.* In order to clarify the situation it may be helpful to summarize some of these.

(1) 'Set' sometimes refers to a pre-aroused expectation of some stimulus features; a readiness to discriminate the colour or shape or to pick out from a perceptual field some particular kind of object.

(2) If a stimulus pattern arouses a gestalt or schema which was not anticipated but which persists throughout a series of perceptions, this is sometimes called a 'set'.

(3) The readiness to react to a stimulus by making or inhibiting a clear-cut response (e.g. pressing a key) is sometimes called a 'set'.

(4) The intention to perform a particular operation is called a 'set'. For example, a series of pairs of numbers is presented and the subject is forewarned to 'add' or 'multiply' or 'subtract'. Or a series of words is presented and the subject responds by giving to each word its contrary meaning, e.g. black – white.

(5) In the course of problem-solving a method or operation, not preconceived or prescribed, emerges out of the activity of problem-solving and is consistently applied. This form of learning – the picking up (by trial and error, or through the operation of positive transfer and generalization) of a skill which has not been taught or practised – is sometimes called a 'set'.

(6) 'Set' sometimes means a tendency to complete a task once

* Gibson, J. J. *Psychological Bulletin*, 1941, p. 781.

it has begun or make a solution as complete and elegant as possible.

(7) 'Set' sometimes means the tendency to go on performing an activity beyond its proper task-situation – a 'fixity' or over-persistence in a given direction.

It may be that these different uses of the word, although describing obviously different functions, are indicative of certain similar mechanisms at work. We do not know anything about these mechanisms, however: they may be the products of learning or they may be produced by special neural mechanisms for coordinating sensory and motor functions. Clearly such 'tendencies', 'readinesses', and 'intentions' have some family resemblance.

The uses of the term 'set' which are most appropriate to the subject of thinking are clearly No. 4, a readiness to perform a previously acquired skill; No. 5, the following of clues arising from a problem and the adaptation of skills to a new need; and No. 6, the tendency to persist at a task until it is accomplished finally. To these three might be added N. R. F. Maier's use of 'set' to mean the direct insight into the structure of a problem resulting from the sudden reorganization of the situation into a new pattern.

Perhaps the meaning which is most obviously relevant to the explanation of the direction and control of thought is one covered by the term 'attitude'. Attitudes or frames of mind can be either conscious or unconscious, either intentions or motor readinesses.

How do such attitudes or sets function in thinking? Motives operate over long periods of time and result in highly varied activities in many different situations. In immediate responses to present stimuli and in moving from one step to another the mechanism of 'set' or 'attitude' is more likely to be at work. Sets operate within brief stretches of behaviour. If we consider any particular moment during a period of activity, the stimuli to which an agent could respond are many and various. But what is selected and attended to is this or that particular object.

Again the number of responses in an agent's repertory is large, but in any specific context the agent is more ready or set to make one particular type of response rather than any others. This may be partly explicable in terms of Hull's habit-hierarchy, but there is still the possibility of using 'set' for the case in which the agent is actively prepared to deal with a specific situation. There is a 'control' present here as contrasted with the situation in which habits are simply tripped off by strong stimulus-objects.

How did the concept of 'set' come into psychology? A brief account of this is worth consideration. It may help to indicate the sort of mechanism involved.

In the years between 1900 and 1914 psychologists working at Würzburg University investigated thinking experimentally for the first time. It had been supposed until then that thought is the product of association of sense contents. One item (sensation or idea) produces the next because of previous contiguity in the experience of the thinker. Marbe studied the reactions of a subject who was required to lift two weights, first simultaneously and then successively, in order to judge which was the heavier. It was found that the subject could not say how the decision came into his thoughts. There were sensations and images but no connexion between these and the final estimate. It was therefore asked, 'What other factors are present to account for the judgement reached?'

It was suggested that 'conscious attitudes' might be the key factor. The Würzburg School now began to investigate attitudes. Since thinking was not directed by simple association these more obscure mechanisms must be the controlling factor in a series of related thoughts.

In 1905 a Scots member of the staff, called Watt, carried out a well-known experiment, using words as stimuli and setting the following tasks to the subjects.

(1) Given a stimulus word that is a species word the subject must name its genus.

(2) Given a species word as stimulus – name a coordinate species.

(3) Given a word naming a whole, respond by naming one of its parts.

(4) Given the name of a part, respond by naming the whole to which it belongs.

(5) Given the name of a part, name another part of the same whole.

Watt asked his subject to report on the contents of consciousness within each of four periods during the experiment. These were: (*a*) a preparatory phase; (*b*) the appearance of the stimulus word; (*c*) the searching for the reaction word; (*d*) the occurrence of the reaction word.

The result of this experiment was that the thought process takes place without any conscious content once the stimulus word is presented, provided that the subject attends during the preparatory period. The first phase is the only significant one – thereafter everything happens automatically. Watt described the conscious task presented in (*a*) as the 'Aufgabe', and it is this which establishes a 'Set' or 'Einstellung' to respond to the stimulus word appropriately. Watt's colleague, Ach, introduced the term 'Determining Tendency' to indicate the fact that the initial 'Aufgabe' carries on to the end of the task and links any habits, associations, etc., previously established into a systematic orderly, purposeful sequence.

Thus with these three concepts – aufgabe, einstellung, and determining tendency – the notion of set was introduced in psychological literature. Some psychologists would be glad to get rid of it altogether, but it is doubtful if this reform is practicable. Some concept, however unsatisfactory its present analysis, seems to be needed in order to indicate the kind of happening which the Würzburg experiments illustrate. 'Set' cannot be used to explain thought – but it is one of the factors at work in the organization and control of a thought process.

D. M. Johnson* discusses the concept of 'set' in detail. He indicates some of the ways in which set arises.

* Johnson, D. M. *The Psychology of Thought and Judgment*. New York (Harper), 1955.

(1) A motive can arouse and maintain specific sets. If X is hungry he will have a set to pick out food sources and his behaviour will be oriented towards seeking, acquiring, and eating should the opportunity occur.

(2) Set is established also by social conditioning. Commands, requests, or instructions lead to clearly defined sets. 'Post this letter if you are going for a walk' or 'Correct the spelling mistakes in these exercises' are sentences which present an 'aufgabe'.

(3) Previously established habits, attitudes, or sets can influence present behaviour. When a man drives off in his car he is ready to react to the movements of other vehicles, to pedestrians, police signals, traffic lights. Maier's experiments have shown how a set established in one task could transfer to a later problem-situation.

(4) Tasks can determine a new set. Skills developed in the past readily generalize into new skills when invoked by a strange task or problem. The task seems to stimulate all the right capacities into coordinated activity.

There are many ways in which set arises and operates as an organizing factor. Set is the key factor in attention and concentration and the selection of appropriate stimuli in the course of a task.

But there are many other organizing and directing factors at work during thinking. Some stimulus might trip off a segment of a habit-hierarchy as the result of previous conditionings, or a random move might lead 'trial and error wise' to the end of a series of operations. But motive and set would seem to be the primary factors which keep the subject on the move and directed towards a specific goal. We do not know very much about motives, and even less about set. But this field of inquiry, although practically unexplored, is clearly that in which the solution to the problem of explaining how thought is directed must be sought.

SELECTED REFERENCES

Gibson, J. J. 'A Critical Review of the Concept of Set in Contemporary Experimental Psychology'. *Psychological Bulletin*, 1941.

Hebb, D. O. *The Organization of Behaviour*. New York (Wiley), 1949.

Johnson, D. M. *The Psychology of Thought and Judgment*. New York and London (Harper), 1955.

McClelland, D. G., Atkinson, J. W., Clark, R. A., and Lowell, E. L. *The Achievement Motive*. New York (Appleton-Century-Crofts), 1953.

Maslow, A. H. *Motivation and Personality*. New York and London (Harper), 1954.

Miller, W. E., and Dollard, J. *Social Learning and Imitation*. New York and London (McGraw-Hill), 1941.

Peters, R. S. 'Motives and Motivation'. *Philosophy*, 1956.

Peters, R. S. *The Concept of Motivation*. London (Routledge), 1958.

CHAPTER NINE

Language and Thought

IT is evident that there is a close connexion between the capacity to use language and the capacities covered by the verb 'to think'. Indeed, some writers have identified thinking with using words: Plato coined the aphorism, 'In thinking the soul is talking to itself'; J. B. Watson reduced thinking to inhibited speech located in the minute movements or tensions of the physiological mechanisms involved in speaking; and although Ryle is careful to point out that there are many senses in which a person is said to think in which words are not in evidence, he has also said that saying something in a specific frame of mind is thinking a thought.

Is thinking reducible to, or dependent upon, language habits? It would seem that many thinking situations are hardly distinguishable from the skilful use of language, although there are some others in which language is not involved. Thought cannot be simply identified with using language. It may be the case, of course, that the non-linguistic skills involved in thought can only be acquired and developed if the learner is able to use and understand language. However, this question is one which we cannot hope to answer in this book. Obviously being able to use language makes for a considerable development in all one's capacities but how precisely this comes about we cannot say.

At the common-sense level it appears that there is often a distinction between thought and the words we employ to communicate with other people. We often have to struggle hard to find words to capture what our thinking has already grasped, and when we do find words we sometimes feel that they fail to do their job properly. Again when we report or describe our thinking to other people we do not merely report unspoken words and sentences. Such sentences do not always occur in thinking, and when they do they are merged with vague imagery and the hint of unconscious or subliminal activities going on just out of range. Thinking, as it happens, is more like struggling, striving, or searching for something than it is like talking or reading. Words do play their part but they are rarely the only feature of thought. This observation is supported by the experiments of the Würzburg psychologists reported in Chapter Eight who showed that intelligent adaptive responses can occur in problem-solving situations without the use of either words or images of any kind. 'Set' and 'determining tendencies' operate without the actual use of language in helping us to think purposefully and intelligently.

Again the study of speech disorders due to brain injury or disease suggests that patients can think without having adequate control over their language. Some patients, for example, fail to find the names of objects presented to them and are unable to describe simple events which they witness; they even find it difficult to interpret long written notices. But they succeed in playing games of chess or draughts.* They can use the concepts needed for chess-playing or draughts-playing but are unable to use many of the concepts in ordinary language. How they manage to do this we do not know. Yet animals such as Köhler's chimpanzees can solve problems by working out strategies such as the invention of implements or climbing aids when such animals have no language beyond a few warning cries. Intelligent or 'insightful' behaviour is not dependent in the case of monkeys on language skills: presumably human beings have various capacities for thinking situations which are likewise independent of language.

Thought cannot simply be identified with language. Yet it is possible that language is a necessary condition for acquiring and developing many drills and skills which are necessary for the sophisticated types of thinking. After all, patients whose capacity to use language is impaired through disease are helpless to per-

* Head, H. *Aphasia and Kindred Disorders of Speech.* Cambridge, 1926.

form many kinds of intellectual work. They cannot write a business letter, organize a team, or prepare and deliver a simple lecture. To what extent is the capacity to think dependent upon the capacity to use language? How do language skills extend the capacity to think and contribute to its characteristics? This is a question which cannot be answered adequately. Nevertheless we can apply what we know about learning (and especially the mediation theory type of explanation which Osgood has developed) to suggest how language works in helping us to think. But what is language? How does the psychologist approach this question?

SIGNS

Language as a means of communication between human beings depends upon uttered noises or writing or gestures. Now, it is sometimes said that when we read a sentence or understand a piece of conversation we are responding to signs. The word 'sign' is used, of course, to refer to many non-verbal sources of stimulation some of which are natural signs and others artificial ones. For example, if I look out of doors and see black clouds piling up I regard these as a sign of rain; if I see a flash of lightning I expect a peal of thunder, or if I feel certain ground movements I expect an earthquake – these are natural signs and we respond to many, less dramatic, specimens every day. When the dinner-gong sounds I go to the dining-room expecting to be served with food, when the red light comes on I halt my car; when the conductor raises his baton I prepare to play from the music score in front of me. These are conventional signs.

Words uttered and written are also a species of sign.

In psychology a sign is defined as a pattern of stimulation which is meaningful – that is, it directs attention to something other than itself (just as the non-verbal signs do): a sign refers to a person, event, or complex situation. Some people want to distinguish different sorts of sign (viz. 'signals', 'symbols') but, for our immediate purposes, it is sufficient to try to define what it is for a pattern of stimulation to function as a sign in language.

Language and Thought

WHAT IS A SIGN?

If a parent asks a child, 'Where is the milk?' and the child begins a search, looking on the doorstep, in the larder, in the refrigerator, etc., we assume that the word 'milk' is meaningful to the child. The word functions as a sign. The child responds to the word by exhibiting appropriate behaviour. It is able to organize and guide its behaviour in relation to something which is not present to perception – it can react in relation to the 'not-here' and 'not-now'.

Now, not all stimuli are meaningful in this way. Not all noises or marks signify something other than themselves. The question to be answered in defining the term 'sign' is: 'Under what conditions does a pattern of stimulation act as a sign of something other than itself and what job does it do when it does so function?'

Osgood has given a plausible answer to this question in the following theory.

Let S=an object, which is any pattern of stimulation which evokes reactions on the part of an organism,

and S=a sign, which is any pattern of stimulation which is not S and yet which evokes reactions relevant to S.

Here S can be anything from a table to a gust of wind, a toothache, or the feel of rain beating down. Also some signs, which Osgood calls 'assigns', say something about other signs or define other signs in some manner.

What is this sign? Take an example: the word PEN (spoken, written, or signalled in morse) is not identical with seeing, touching, handling a particular specimen with which one writes. Yet the use of the sign does elicit behaviour which is, in some way, related to the object. Other stimulus patterns do not function as a word such as 'pen' does. How does this come about?

In the first place, the use of the sign 'pen' has to be learned. Neither human beings nor any other living creatures are born with an innate capacity to respond to stimuli as signs. What is it, in the field of learned skills, which makes for a pattern of stimulation coming to be a sign?

If X asks Y: 'Bring me a pen', Y responds by looking in drawers and cupboards until the search produces a particular specimen of the class of objects which Y then brings to X. Y has responded to a pattern of auditory stimuli functioning as a sign.

How does this differ from X stepping to his front-door, looking at the black clouds, and going out armed with umbrella and mackintosh? Or how does it differ from our familiar friends the rats who learn to anticipate an electric shock by turning a ratchet whenever a buzzer sounds five seconds before the electricity comes on?

Is there anything in common between these three sign-situations? Osgood suggests that it is the presence or absence of a representational mediating response in association with the stimulus which explains how a sign comes to do the work it does.

We have already discussed the mediation hypothesis in Chapter Six. To restate this, very briefly:

Some complexes of stimuli elicit particular sequences of behaviour without mediation. These are stimulus objects: S.

Others, however, elicit mediation processes: these are signs: S.

An object S elicits certain sequences of behaviour. A second pattern of stimulation S will – given suitable conditions of reinforcement – arouse some fraction of the total response-sequence originally elicited by the object. This fraction is the representational mediation process, and it may be a muscular or glandular reaction. In human subjects it may have a conscious outcome – a shiver-feeling as the dark sky is noticed, a sinking ache of apprehension as one hears the air-raid siren, vague kinaesthetic tensions associated with writing when one hears or reads the word 'pen'. Whether or not there is a conscious basis or even a muscular or glandular reaction which can be located does not matter. Some reaction is the fraction, the representational mediating factor. This, in its turn, serves as a stimulus for the overt response to the sign – it mediates in such a way that the response to the sign is independent of the behaviour elicited by the object which is referred to by the sign. The representational mediating response – itself a fragment of the original total response elicited by the object – is not the final response to the sign: it merely sets off that response.

In a sense, the mediating response is the basis for the meaning of the sign.

To take two examples, given by Osgood, to illustrate this theory of meaning. The word 'hammer' stands for a familiar piece of carpenter's equipment. When a child learns to name this object he knows that it names a thing to be grasped, wielded, and used in certain ways. The muscular and nervous reactions involved in actually using a hammer supply the fraction of the detachable behaviour which serves as a mediating response connecting sign to object. A young child when asked to find a hammer often moves its arm up and down in a 'hammering' mime when searching for the absent object. This is a specimen in which the extensional use of the sign is emphasized.

To consider another example in which the intensional meaning is emphasized. Suppose somebody says during a picnic, 'There is a SNAKE in that grass'. This may produce distinctive reactions – feelings of anxiety and distaste and defensive-protective stances. How does this come about?

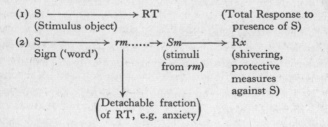

Originally the stimulus object S – actual presence of a snake – elicits a pattern of behaviour (RT) which includes fear and apprehension. Through short-circuiting (familiar in many learning situations) detachable portions of this total behaviour to S become conditioned to the word 'snake'. These fragments are what we mean by anxiety and dislike. With repetitions the representational mediation process becomes reduced to a minimum. In a summer picnic the word arouses much more activity than it does when mentioned in a drawing-room reminiscence on a winter evening – although there may still be faint anxiety and positive dislike aroused which give the word an 'unpleasant' connotation even in the security of the fireside circle.

There is also an important family of signs called 'assigns', the meaning of which is 'assigned' to them through association, not with the objects they are used to discuss but with other signs. We can consider dodos or the doings of the ancient Egyptians without ever having had direct dealings with either of these long since extinct beings. We can do this because the terms can be defined by using other signs the meaning of which we learn in the way already described. The way in which complex words are established is a subject which we do not need to discuss here. Obviously it is one of great importance. In the case of the dodo it is sufficient to point out to somebody who does not know what a dodo was that it was an 'animal' (sign already learned), which was a kind of bird (sign) rather like a swan (sign) which could not fly (sign) and which was 'short-legged', 'clumsy', etc., etc. Familiar signs can make the task of giving the meaning of the 'assign' easy. When it comes to abstract terms such as 'time', 'number', 'cause', etc., the job of giving an account of how such signs work becomes more complicated but not essentially different – we have to show: (*a*) how they are learned; (*b*) what function they characteristically serve in communication.

There are obviously many different kinds of sign – each with its own typical work to do.

So much for single signs – simple patterns of stimulation that direct our attention to physical objects such as tables or pens, simple events such as 'fires' or 'explosions', or to persons. In even the simplest communication, however, sentences are used in which signs are deployed and re-deployed in such a way that we can respond to a very wide range of situations. A sentence never previously heard or read can be understood immediately and can thus serve as a stimulus for a complex response-sequence. New situations can be met successfully or anticipated through the use of the sign situation in which the sentence is the unit rather than the single sign. How do sentences work in communication? O. H. Mowrer has recently suggested how a simple indicative sentence may function as a conditioning device in controlling behaviour.

THE SENTENCE AS A CONDITIONING DEVICE

In his paper 'A Psychologist Looks at Language',* O. H. Mowrer suggests that the sentence can often operate as a conditioning device, a means of changing a person's pattern of behaviour. Indeed, one of the tests for finding out whether or not a sentence has communicated information from X to Y is any relevant modifications in Y's behaviour.

To use Mowrer's own example:

Suppose X says to Y, 'Tom is a thief': this produces a conditioning situation.

(a) 'Tom'⟶'thief'⟶$rt.$ (b) 'Tom'——$rt.$

Y now reacts to the name 'Tom' (or to the actual presence of the person named) in a different way than he did before. Part of the reactions to the concept 'thief' become attached to this total response to the person called 'Tom' (suspicion, mistrust). The sentence thus works as a conditioning device in that its job is to produce new associations (new learning) which lead the subject to make changes in his behaviour. Once the sentence is accepted as true or probable Y's treatment of Tom changes. But how exactly does all this happen? How through the use of words does Y come to change his behaviour towards the presence of Tom? Mowrer believes that this change can be explained solely by reference to simple learning operations. His explanation runs as follows:

* *American Psychologist.* November 1954.

Stage 1. First we have to explain how the words 'Tom' and 'thief' acquire their meaning for Y.

'Tom' gets its meaning by being associated with and occurring in actual contexts in which Y meets Tom as a person.

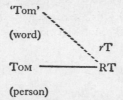

$$\text{'Tom'} \diagdown$$
$$\text{(word)}$$
$$r\text{T}$$
$$\text{TOM} \text{———} \text{RT}$$
$$\text{(person)}$$

The actual presence of TOM evokes the complex reaction RT of which rT is a fragment (visual impression, emotional reaction!) This detachable reaction rT gets shifted from TOM to 'Tom' as a result of the paired presentation of TOM and his name word. Consider what happens to animals in conditioning experiments of the form:

Buzzer—shock—pain, fear, escape movements (RT, total

$$\underset{(r\text{T})}{|} \qquad \text{reaction including } r\text{T}).$$

Buzzer—anxiety, fear......(rT, detachable bit of RT).

Similarly with the word 'thief':
    'thief'
        (word)

$$rt$$

THIEF .... Rt 'thief...............rt.
(actual person who steals)

It may be noted that the word 'thief' might not be learned by the subject observing a thief at work. Instead he might be admonished during childhood training not to take things which do not belong to him. Thus the word 'thief' functions here as an assign, a sign which has its meaning assigned to it through its associations with other signs rather than through being associated with a particular event. However, this difference does not alter the validity of the above conditioning paradigm.

Thus when the sentence 'Tom is a thief' is used, the rt reaction gets shifted from the word 'thief' to the word 'Tom'. But with what consequences? Does the word 'Tom' become synonymous with the word 'thief'? This is obviously not the case. The change is a far subtler one. What this change might be Mowrer goes on to suggest as follows.

Stage 2. Consider the conventional model for conditioning.

$$CS \dashrightarrow R?$$
$$UCS \text{——} UCR.$$

If we substitute the example we have been considering, we get:

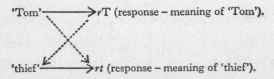

'Tom' $\longrightarrow rT$ (response – meaning of 'Tom').

'thief' $\longrightarrow rt$ (response – meaning of 'thief').

Here the well-established conditional response rT to the conditional stimulus (a factor usually left out in Pavlovian conditioning) plays an important part as a mediating reaction. This factor influences the total learning situation. To remodel the above:

(a) 'Tom' $\longrightarrow rT$ (b) 'Tom' $\text{——} rT \text{——} rt$

      'thief' $\longrightarrow rt$

The 'Tom' $\text{——} rT$ conditioning is a stable one. Thus when the word 'Tom' and the word 'thief' are paired in the sentence 'Tom is a thief', the mediating response rT becomes associated with *rt* as above. Thus when Y next meets Tom in person the following situation arises:

$$\text{'Tom'} \longrightarrow r\text{T} \longrightarrow rt$$

$$\text{TOM} \longrightarrow \text{RT} \quad \overset{(r\text{T})}{\longrightarrow} rt$$

Since *r*T is a component of RT from the very beginning of Stage 1 it follows that the *r*T serves as a mediating response between this original response and all the conditionings effected through the word-meanings. Y now treats TOM with mistrust and caution (even if he conceals this from Tom). A new association has been formed to (part of) his original complex response to Tom as a person.

What work, then, does this sentence perform, considered as a conditioning device? As Mowrer points out, it might be used as the basis of a simple syllogism:

> Thieves cannot be trusted.
> Tom is a thief
> ∴ Tom cannot be trusted.

This achieves a change in classification. Tom has hitherto been a member of the class of honest or trustworthy men. Now he is removed from this class and placed in the class of thieves. Although mediation is needed for this simple deduction this situation is not unlike that of the simple conditioning experiment which leaves out the mediation and in which the conditional stimulus takes on some of the attributes of the unconditional stimulus. (A painful pairing bell-with-shock makes the bell an anxiety-provoking sign, whereas bell-with-food makes the bell a food-anticipatory-response provoking sign.) Thus the sentence, effecting conditioning, serves as the basis of elementary deductive reasoning.

Furthermore, conditioning through the sentence helps us to make simple plans for future action. If I repeat several times to myself, 'The next time I am in Grainger Street I must turn off

into the closed market and buy some cat-food at the Pet Store'
it may happen that several days later I find myself walking along
Grainger Street on my way from the railway station to the college. While walking along the street I suddenly remember cat-
food – market, and accordingly go off my route to do the shop-
ping. I have conditioned myself in advance to react to the sight
of Grainger Street by remembering the market, the store, and
the purchase to be made there.

Now in both these examples two steps are made by using the
sentence.

(1) The subject-predicate sentence leads to a 'transfer' of
meaning from one sign to another sign; this is effected through
conditioning.

(2) There is a further 'transfer' of meaning from a sign to its
referent, a thing, person, or event. This comes about through
generalization.

The sentence does its job, in modifying behaviour, by effecting
an associative shift whereby responses directed towards the
referent of the subject term of the sentence are modified. First
the meaning of the subject term of the sentence is modified
through conditioning, and then, through generalization, the
behaviour of the person who accepts the sentence is changed in
relation to whatever the subject term of the sentence refers to.
A mediation response is needed to effect this shift; how this
comes about may be understood from earlier discussions of
mediation in Chapter Six and from Osgood's account of how
signs acquire meaning earlier in this chapter. Once a system of
mediating responses has been acquired it is easier to grasp the
principle that categorizing is possible and that class can be related to class in various ways. Classification may be regarded as
the product of generalization of response from sign to each X
which is a member of the class. Elementary forms of deductive
reasoning can proceed on the basis of the relations of class inclusion and exclusion. Without the sentence, considered as a conditioning and generalizing device, elementary reasoning could
not be carried out with efficiency and clarity. Perhaps visual and

other imagery might be used instead of words but images are less capable of control and are more ambiguous as signs. In their extensional use at least, words are relatively definite and fixed, whereas images are vague, changeable, and less capable of being separated from intensional uses; furthermore, they are not public and are therefore incapable of being given conventional definition. Of course, this example involves a simple indicative sentence which is used in a highly specific situation. One cannot generalize from the way in which one sentence operates psychologically to change behaviour. There are many different sorts of sentence which perform different kinds of job. In any case, to confine attention to communication between two people might now throw much light on language in relation to thought processes.

Nevertheless it is possible to put forward a few suggestions concerning the function of languages in thinking.

The use of signs, even at the rudimentary level of the simple indicative sentence, makes for the possibility of a greater degree of awareness than otherwise might be the case. We are able to fixate, isolate, and then relate aspects of what otherwise might be a confused complex, through being able to use signs. We give names and descriptions to persons, things, and events which recur in our perceptual experience. Thus the environment, quite early in life, becomes meaningful at every glance. Although we do not use words when we perceive the world, it is in virtue of having learned to name, describe, and relate what is commonly perceived that we come to know a structured, consistent, and ordered world. Language assists us to build up a detailed and understood map of the world we inhabit. It may be that some animals, such as chimpanzees or dogs, have some grasp of the order of things. However, the behaviour of most animals suggests that they are much more at the mercy of immediate stimuli and that what they perceive trips off an appropriate habit to an extent which is rare with human beings. Human beings treat the world more abstractly and gain some degree of detachment from the concrete present.

Again, since elementary deduction may be regarded as operating with explicit regard to class relationships, elementary reasoning may derive from the ability to use a complex system of signs. It is possible that visual imagery might enable a person to do what is generally more easily done by constructing and testing the validity of syllogisms. But surely the deliberate manipulation of class concepts through the use of signs is much more economical and efficient? The subject-predicate sentence form provides one way in which these class relationships may be handled. Further, language enables us to make precise requests and demands and thus helps us to organize all kinds of information in easily codifiable forms. A person can learn to tackle and solve new problems and acquire new skills because the other people can quickly communicate facts and show him what to do. Language makes for greater control and economy in the development and application of intelligent behaviour.

Some sentences mention individual persons, things, or events and describe what exists and happens in the world in a direct fashion. Other sentences, however, do not mention particulars but refer, in summary indirect fashion, to an unspecified range of particulars. Such abstract or general sentences often convey a great deal of information, nevertheless. For example, 'The Church has consistently opposed divorce'; 'The British are no longer prepared to work hard'; 'Football has been played in Brazil since 1905'. When we say something about the attitude of the Church we refer indirectly to the outcome of the discussions, debates, resolutions of a number of individual persons over a great many years which have resulted in the leaders and followers of the present Church organization tending to hold certain opinions rather than others. This sort of sentence is only at one level of abstractness above straightforward descriptions or statements. But there are many more types of sentence (e.g. those containing words such as 'if', 'then', 'because', 'therefore') whose function is much more complicated. Such complex sentence-forms can only be used by people who have learned to use simpler and less abstract types of sentence. Since reasoning involves the use of the more abstract types of sentence, it pre-supposes as one of its necessary conditions the existence of a complex system of signs. Without being able to use language intelligently, thought at the most abstract level seems impossible.

The word 'abstract' has been used several times. It has been used to distinguish between sentences which attempt to deal directly with whatever we observe and sentences which are de-rived from such descriptive statements. However, the ability to view the world abstractly is more general than this and may not be a function of using signs. Goldstein and Scheerer,* two psy-chologists who have studied the psychological effects of damage to the brain in injury and disease, believe that abstraction is a unique functional level of activity. As a result of many tests, de-signed to discover the degree of impairment of mental function suffered by brain-damaged cases, they make a crucial distinction between two levels of behaviour. One is the *concrete* level to which most brain-damaged cases are confined; the other is the *abstract* which together with the concrete is part of every normal person's general capacity. The difference between these two types of behaviour is best illustrated by describing certain defi-ciencies suffered by the patients.

Normal people display a certain detachment from their en-vironmental situation and also from their inner moods, inclina-tions, and motivational states. Patients suffering from brain injury lose this detachment. A female patient if asked to bring a comb from a table and hand it to a psychologist could not do this without actually combing her hair. Another patient when asked to repeat the false statement, 'Snow is black' could only respond by saying 'No, it is white'.

Normal people can easily assume all kinds of 'set'. A patient could tell the time when shown a clock but could not set the hands of the clock to a stated time. If a normal person is required to recite the alphabet and is interrupted he can pick up the task at the point at which he left off but patients typically can only continue if they start at the beginning again.

* Goldstein, K. and Scheerer, M. 'Abstract and Concrete Be-haviour'. *Psychological Monograph*, 53, No. 2, 1941.

If such patients are given very simple arithmetical problems (addition and subtraction of small numbers) they can use their fingers to solve them. But when asked, 'Is 7 a bigger number than 4?' they cannot answer such a question. Analogies and metaphors of the simplest kind are frequently lost on such patients. Moreover, patients who can find their own way about a maze of hospital buildings without difficulty are unable to direct other people from one point to another or even to describe how they have come from one point to another.

Goldstein and Scheerer have devised many simple tests involving the sorting of wooden blocks of various shapes, sizes, and colours into groups on the basis of simple principles (e.g. on basis of colour differences). Normal people find such tests extremely easy but brain-damaged patients find great difficulty in doing them at all.

The patients are efficient when operating at the concrete level but they cannot operate at the abstract level. They cannot detach themselves from the functional and practical properties of a present situation and consider it in relation to past events or future possibilities or other factors in the environment which do not have an *obvious* and immediate relation to whatever it is with which they are concerned. The ability to do what these patients *cannot* do covers a very wide range of activities. Goldstein and Scheerer believe that the difference between the two levels is a radical one. A new functional level comes into operation at the abstract level and this may involve the healthy operation of certain parts of the brain which are relatively inactive at the concrete level of behaviour.

What is interesting to notice is that the patients can use language properly. They respond appropriately to commands, requests, questions, and instructions, and they can communicate to other people in a variety of ways. They cannot think at the abstract level, however. One of the necessary conditions for thinking is absent, although the ability to use language is not destroyed. The Goldstein and Scheerer patients are the contrary case to the patients mentioned earlier in the chapter who have lost the ability to use language to a considerable extent and yet who can play chess or draughts with some skill. The ability to think is not identical with the ability to use language. Without language some people can still display considerable intellectual powers and with language relatively intact other people are unable to think at all efficiently.

Psychologists are unable to explain such facts. What is the explanation of the difference between concrete and abstract levels and how the range of capacities at each level is related to skill in the use of language are questions which cannot be answered at present. It is unlikely that any *one* set of psychological functions is responsible for either the capacity to operate at the abstract level or the capacity to develop the use of signs for a wide variety of jobs.

CONCLUSION

No doubt human intelligence – all the capacities, skills, dispositions, and insights which constitute thought – are largely a function of what is summarily referred to by such terms as 'perception', 'learning', 'motivation', and 'abstraction'. Nevertheless, without language as developed and used by human beings few skills could originate and develop beyond the crude trial and error stage analogous to that exhibited by chimpanzees or children during their sensori-motor period.

Thinking cannot, it is suggested, be reduced simply to learning and using the system of signs called 'language'. When a human being is described as 'thinking' he may be doing any one of a number of quite different things. Sometimes these activities are largely a matter of using lanaguage but sometimes not. Ryle has suggested that much thinking is not so much a case of having words in mind as 'rummaging for and finding, or failing to find, words'. Language is not the only factor involved in thinking. Nevertheless much abstract thought would be impossible without the thinker having learned to use a complex system of signs with care and skill. Reasoning of the most rigorous kind involves: (*a*) much learning dependent on the use of language for its existence; (*b*) the actual use of complex signs.

How could the Würzburg experiments which demonstrated the possibility of imageless and wordless thought have taken place without the use of language? The subject had to be given verbal instructions by the experimenter in order to know what to do, the experimenter was dependent upon the verbal reports of his subjects for his results, and part of the experiments involved word-association tests. Most higher-level thought is dependent on language and is largely a matter of using language intelligently in relation to whatever one is considering, but not all thought is of this kind. Some thinking is more closely related to imaginative activity than to logical or scientific activity.

Perhaps the greatest influence of language on thought is a matter of social psychology. Information and advice based on the accumulated discoveries of previous generations can be codified and transmitted in speech and writing and thus added to the experience of the individual. Educational institutions function very large through the use and development of language and contribute to the elaboration and refinement of the uses of language. Anyone who has gone to school and college ought to have developed his system of signs very considerably as a result of his special training. Yet the student does not merely increase his ability to use words or other symbols. He develops a wide range of intelligent capacities and habits during the course of formal education. Without being able to use a highly complex system of signs, however, it is unlikely that any of these higher skills could be acquired and strengthened.

Thus the study of language is an integral part of the study of thinking. Unfortunately psychologists have little to offer. The study of language by psychologists has only been undertaken on a wide scale since the end of the Second World War and so far their studies have been exploratory. Very little empirical work has been carried out and it is difficult to think how experiments could be designed which would adequately investigate such a complex skill. It may be that psychologists will have to depend on experts outside of their subject for the materials out of which a psychology of language can be made. Semantics, linguistics, analytical philosophy, and communication theory are studies which have developed considerably in recent years. It may be that psychologists will borrow ideas from these other specialists and so construct theories which will enable us to give more satisfactory answers to questions concerning the relationship between thought and language.

SELECTED REFERENCES

Carroll, J. B. *The Study of Language*. Chapter 3. New York (Harvard Press), 1953.

Henle, P. *Language, Thought and Culture*. Ann Arbor (Michigan University Press), 1958.

Humphrey, G. *Thinking*. Chapter 8. London (Methuen), 1951.

Lewis, M. M. *Infant Speech*. London (Kegan Paul), 1936.

Lewis, M. M. *How Children Learn to Speak*. London (Harrap), 1957.

Miller, G. A. *Language and Communication*. New York (McGraw-Hill), 1953.

Morris, C. R. *Signs, Language and Behaviour*. New York (Prentice-Hall), 1946.

Mowrer, O. H. 'A Psychologist Looks at Language'. *American Psychologist*, November 1954.

Osgood, C. E. *Method and Theory in Experimental Psychology*. Chapter 16. Oxford, 1953.

Osgood, C. E., Suci, G. J., and Tannenbaum, P. H. *The Measurement of Meaning*. Urbana (Illinois University Press), 1957.

Ryle, G. 'Thinking and Language'. *Proceedings of the Aristotelian Society*, 1951.

CHAPTER TEN

Creative Thinking

So far we have been concerned either with the conditions of thought – learning operations, motivational states, language habits, or else with typical situations which involve thought processes – forming and attaining concepts, acquiring strategies and improving tactics in specific 'problem-situations', and the like. All this may well appear to be missing the essential; attending to desiccated anatomical specimens of thought rather than to the activity of thinking as we experience it.

Thinking is one of the most remarkable of human achievements. In most countries the creative thinker, whether scientist or poet, is rightly acclaimed and respected, while even the ordinary mortal gets some satisfaction out of winning scholarships and prizes, from passing examinations, or even from working out chess and crossword puzzles; from any activity, in fact, which tests intelligence and imagination.

We want to know what it is that human beings do when they engage in creative thinking. How is it that some people can produce novels, plays, musical compositions, or paintings? How can certain scientists create striking and fruitful hypotheses and then devise the most ingenious experimental methods to test the truth of these? What is it that makes for mathematical genius or philosophical acumen?

And quite apart from such outstanding minds, what is it that makes a sound research chemist, a good schoolmaster, or a bright script-writer for TV or sound broadcasting? How do they manage it while the rest of us muddle along in our confused and pedestrian fashion?

Obviously such creativity is known by its works. Creative thinking results in products (poems, pictures, experiments, learned articles, etc.), the quality of which makes us call them 'original', 'creative', or 'imaginative'. The layman is apt to believe that the thought processes and activities which result in the admirable product must be quite exceptional – utterly different from those which he indulges in through the humdrum routine of his everyday life. But is this really the case? Is the creative thinker a special kind of man or only a man whom special training, skill, and the acquisition of a personal style have made somewhat more competent than others? Most of us can run, after a fashion: the Olympic champions excel the ordinary untrained man when it comes to athletic running – but then how much of their performance is due to instruction, training, exercise, special incentives? Perhaps few of us if given the chance could ever match a really great runner – but who knows? So, too, the ordinary man might produce creatively if he were given favourable conditions under which to develop his hidden powers and talents.

Is the original thinker merely the product of privileged development, or has he some 'gift' in his make-up which makes him different from ordinary people? Psychologists cannot give a satisfactory answer to this interesting question in the present state of their subject. Nevertheless, some tentative suggestions can be put forward to fill this gap in our knowledge.

There are at least three questions which a psychologist would set up as goals towards which his thinking ought to move:

(1) What do we mean by 'creative thinking'? The notion is ambiguous. There are clearly differences between the genius and the average performer, e.g. between Beethoven and the successful composer of musical comedies. Also there are differences between different species of productivity – between painting and mathematics, science and poetry, music and military strategy. Many different conditions, different skills, capacities and aptitudes, motives and needs are involved in different kinds of creativity. Yet it is possible that there are important similarities between the different species and it may be that similar principles of thought and action are involved.

(2) What is it that makes for different degrees of excellence in

creative thinking? What makes Beethoven greater than Sullivan? Some unknown factors in personality? Social conditions? Specific training?

(3) What are the conditions in which creative thinking occurs and which seem to influence its course? Are these similar in the different arts and sciences? What do people *do* when they think creatively?

We cannot hope to answer the first two of these questions and it is futile to attempt to do so here. We can, however, say something relevant in answer to the third question. We can describe the kind of activity which goes on during some species of creativity and the conditions which seem essential for that activity. This is a gesture on the part of psychology in response to the layman's demand that he be told something straightforward about a familiar psychological function!

THE CREATIVE SITUATION

As Vinacke and others have pointed out, most actual thinking alternates between two poles, which we may call the Realistic and the Imaginative. The realistic involves adhering fairly strictly to logical and scientific criteria and being tied in one's responses to the external situation; reason and facts dominate one's field. The imaginative pole allows inner currents to play with data originally provided by perception. In imaginative activity the subject experiments, fairly freely, with his data and throws up hypotheses, suggestions, fantasies, images, and comparisons, and often strives towards unclear and barely conceived goals.

In successful thinking, organization and control – the logical discipline of the realistic altitude – are necessary. But the wilder, vaguer imaginative roving is also needed: it has its own contribution to make to the total activity.

Thus there is a switching from one pole to the other and much intermediate 'mixing' of the two styles or attitudes in actual thought processes.

This distinction, as it stands, is abstract and rather crude. The best corrective is a consideration of concrete examples.

THE ARTIST AND THE WAY HE WORKS

In an interesting book, *The Creative Process*, edited by Brewster Ghiselin, a number of creative thinkers discuss the way they think when engaged in making a poem, a novel, a painting, or in mathematical discovery or scientific research. Also Peter McKellar, of Sheffield University, in his book, *Imagination and Thinking*, has a chapter on the conditions of creativity in which he uses many striking examples from 'life'.

Mr Stephen Spender in 'The Making of a Poem' (reproduced in Ghiselin) gives a clear account of what is involved in his work. He makes a distinction between the clear, sharp intuition which is the conception of the poem and the systematic plodding job of working out what the intuition has hinted. The poet has to work, like most of us when doing intellectual jobs, from rough draft to formulation, from formulation to revised version, from revised version to a copy corrected in the light of 'second thoughts'. Spender puts down promising ideas in note-books and draws on these when working. He gets an idea – a mere line, phrase, or even a single word – which is moving and impelling. This is the start: the intuition. This appears to be active and germinal, as if it had to grow into a fully written poem. 'Everything is work except inspiration,' says Spender. The detail has to be worked out painfully and the poem presents itself as a series of problems to which the poet must apply his intelligence and his techniques as a writer. Skill at using language and cultivating sensitivity is largely a matter of experience, training, and deliberate hard work. Spender works over his material with care and thought, and sometimes has to draft a set of lines some twenty to thirty times before he is satisfied that they are the completed version of the 'dim cloud of an idea' which has at last been 'condensed ... in words'. Spender also says that although much hard work goes into a poem, nevertheless at its centre is a deeply personal experience, in which something of the poet's individuality is expressed. His talent is uniquely his, and in being judged as a poet the writer is being judged as a man.

Thus the creation of poetry involves the disciplined application of skills and techniques to a specific problem-situation – sheer hard work: but there is also the striking experience of 'inspiration'; the sudden emergence of a germ of thought which catches the writer's interest and seems to demand exploitation into a finished product at the hands of the artist. The involvement of the artist is also mentioned by Spender: he talks of the intense physical and nervous excitement and sense of release which accompanies work on a poem.

This intensity is mentioned by several other writers. Dorothy Canfield, the novelist, asserts that her creative work begins with a general intensification of emotion in which quite typical everyday events become capable of moving her quite deeply. In such a mood any event – an expression seen on someone's face, their tone of voice, a single sentence overheard in a conversation between strangers – serves as a centre round which the idea for a story develops. Once this idea begins to formulate the rest is a problem to be worked out by hard thinking. Plots have to be sketched, experimented with, modified, and half-abandoned before a novel is worked out and written down. The pattern is similar to that for the poet: heightened sensitivity, a germinal idea 'given' out of the blue, and a period of hard work in which the writer's ingenuity is tested in a series of definable 'problem situations'.

Nor are poets and novelists the only ones to experience this kind of pattern. Henri Poincaré has described a piece of original work in mathematics. Poincaré was trying to prove that there could not be any functions like those which are called Fuchsian functions. Every day for a considerable period he worked on a great number of combinations but failed to reach any results. One evening he drank black coffee before lying down to sleep. He failed to get a restful night, but he was subject to an experience which was nevertheless welcome. Ideas rose in crowds in his restless head: he appeared to be a spectator of a number of 'hooked atoms' which combined and re-combined in one combination after another. In the morning, almost in spite of any effort on his part, the solution to his problem had been grasped. Poincaré was able, after two hours of concentrated work, to set out the proof he was seeking.

As a result of this, Poincaré set down the conditions of creativity.

(1) First a period of conscious work. The data are assembled, the problem defined, and some trials are made at solution.

(2) Next the unconscious gets to work. What happens is that useful and fertile combinations are selected and useless ones are inhibited. But how does this take place? Is there a subconscious working out of all possible combinations resulting in the publication (to consciousness) of those only which are appropriate for the specific problem? Or is it a matter of chance which combinations are selected? We do not know. What is certain is that only those hypotheses which are relevant emerge, and that there is a conscious reaction to these which is distinctive. An appropriate hypothesis strikes the thinker with its aesthetic properties, much as a good work of art does. Aesthetic sensibility is the clue to the soundness of a hypothesis.

(3) Finally, the hypothesis gives merely a hint or direction to be followed – not the completed proof. The proof has to be worked out by the application of mathematical ingenuity. This may take time and effort and involve the solution of quite difficult problems.

Here again there is the pattern of intuition followed by hard work and the application of learned techniques.

EXPERIMENTAL INVESTIGATION

We have now some information about what the creative thinker does when at work, derived from reports by actual practitioners.

Attempts to produce the conditions of creativity in the laboratory have not proved successful. The only research which is worth reporting was undertaken in the 1930s by Patrick. It does not provide any startling results, but it tends to confirm the general picture which a reading of Ghiselin's book provides.

The activities studied by Patrick were the writing of a poem, the painting of a picture, and the solving of a scientific problem. The subjects were divided into two groups – one consisting of trained professionals and the other of non-specialists. Care was taken to make the two groups homogeneous with regard to age, intelligence, and sex.

Each subject was given a stimulus object in response to which he was to engage in activity: the poets were given a landscape painting as a stimulus and the painters were presented with a poem by John Milton.

While they worked the subjects were encouraged to talk about their task, their problems, and their inclinations about tackling it. Experimenters observed and reported their activity, aided by recording machines.

There was no time-limit, and at the end of each session a questionnaire was given to each subject on 'methods and problems of work'. One of the general conclusions which Patrick drew from the data was that creative thinking proceeds through a series of stages.

Preparation. Here the subject makes himself familiar with his situation and its materials.

Incubation. The problem begins to be defined. Suggestions occur, and fragments of the final product appear.

Illumination. A specific goal is envisaged and the subject begins to work towards it.

Verification. The results are worked out fully, revised, altered, completed. (Testing – in case of hypothesis.)

Other investigations tend to confirm Patrick's findings. Only one modification has been suggested: namely, that the four phases of activity do not necessarily occur in a well-defined sequence. There is sometimes a sudden continuous movement which embraces all phases in one: or else the thinker may work backwards and forwards over the four 'phases' before suddenly winding-up with a flourish. Thinking is a dynamic, intense, and highly personal activity which cannot be tied down to any formula or pattern which fits any individual case. Some creative thinkers are systematic, orderly, thorough, and apply their techniques with deliberate purpose: others follow impulse from start to finish and give 'inspired' performances. Stephen Spender illustrated two contrasting types in Mozart and Beethoven: the former 'intuitive' writing his music as it came to him and the latter struggling from a pitifully weak idea to a great masterpiece after days of toil and anxiety.

The former, says Spender, is like a man who dives suddenly into the depths of an experience: the latter is one who digs deeper and deeper, layer by layer, towards the heart of his experience. For many artists there is a middle way involving both styles of thinking.

These experiments do not really show us anything that we did not know before. Their chief merit is simply to suggest that the ordinary man works in a similar style to some great artists in dealing with creative tasks.

THE CONDITIONS OF CREATIVE THINKING

We can now summarize some of the conditions which appear to influence creativity.

THE IMPORTANCE OF PREPARATION

Without collecting, selecting, and analysing data and without some preliminary trial and error at one's task, creative activity is unlikely to be productive. 'A period of preliminary conscious work ... always precedes all fruitful unconscious work' (Poincaré). No intuitions will come without prior hard work. For the poet this also involves a prior education in reading, observing, travelling, and practising the art of writing; for the scientist, submitting to a long training and to minor researches; for the painter, studying the work of other artists. And then, for each of these, the survey of each specific task-situation is essential.

INCUBATION

There must also be a period of incubation during which the thinker is not consciously concerned about his task. The data assimilated during the preparation period seem to sort themselves out below the range of consciousness. Since Freud, it is not difficult to accept the notion that a human being is often active in a purposeful way 'unconsciously'. And also to accept the sudden emergence in consciousness of the result of this unconscious activity as a normal psychological function.

We do not know what happens during this phase or how the unconscious works. No doubt the material assimilated is restructured by changes in associative connexions, but how this takes place and why we have this phase occurring at all is a matter for speculation.

We merely know that this phenomenon does occur. We suddenly get the solution to a long-struggled-for problem: or we wake up after sleep with the idea we had been working for all the previous evening.

PRIOR LEARNING

The creative thinker, however fortunate in his intuitions, must have learned thoroughly a considerable range of skills, habits, and capacities without which he could not begin to work. Much of his work must come effortlessly to him: all great artists, mathematicians, and scientists are masters of techniques which can only be acquired after long and patient training. The painter has learned all about colour-mixing and brushwork and anatomy before he gets down to his specific task of painting a Madonna. The musician has mastered harmony, counterpoint, orchestration, and composition long before he sets a libretto to music.

At the same time over-practice of some skill may produce rigidity and over-emphasis. The professor of mathematics, who has helped to advance his subject, may never learn to operate a Sten gun when enlisted in the wartime Home Guard. And the practical man of affairs may fail to understand some important statistical analysis which would help him greatly to plan his business; one's training must be thorough and at one's finger-tips, but appropriate and flexible, capable of transfer to new problems.

It is sometimes argued that the condition which favours most the transfer of prior learning in creativity is that in which there is a maximum interaction between primary and secondary perception. Primary perception may be defined as one's own first-hand experience of life, and secondary perception what one has acquired from reading, training, formal instruction, etc. The free interaction of the products of primary and secondary perception, however this may be effected, provides a melting-pot out of which original thought boils up.

SENSORY CUES

It is known that original thinkers often need some highly specific stimulus to aid them in their periods of activity. Kant used a tower, seen through his bedroom window, as a focus when concentrating on metaphysical topics. Schiller kept rotten apples in his desk – apparently the smell stimulated him when writing verse and drama. Stephen Spender remarked that he finds coffee and tobacco indispensable stimulants while writing, while W. H. Auden prefers tea. Freud's friends, in time of short-age, were careful to hoard cheroots – deprived of a supply of this type of tobacco the great psycho-analyst might have worked less efficiently or perhaps not at all!

Such conditions are more important than might be supposed. The thinker's physical situation is a narrowly prescribed one and every factor in it may contribute to his state. Just as certain sensory stimuli are needed for well-being, so too certain other stimuli may be annoying or distracting. Such disturbances may be quite a problem in our overcrowded, noise-shattered urban centres.* Granted the presence and persistence of certain sensory cues, creative thought for certain people might be impossible.

* See 'How Much Can Our Nerves Stand?' in Michael Roberts, *The Estate of Man*, London (Faber), 1951.

Creative Thinking

As McKellar has pointed out, personality structure determines the style and approach of different types of thinker.

We are all familiar with the iconoclast, the destructive critic who seems primarily interested in attacking and destroying other people's theories. Such thinkers often do some useful work in discrediting superstition and charlatanry and in exposing weakness in generally accepted hypotheses. Nevertheless such critics may not be creative thinkers: they do not make important discoveries or introduce stimulating innovations.

Again, there are the intellectual diehards who defend established traditions in their field of interest. The classical example of such thinkers is that of the medieval scholars who 'worshipped rather than studied' Aristotle. Aristotle was appealed to as an ultimate authority and his views were treated as dogmas. If anything conflicted with what Aristotle had said, then it must be wrong. Instead of following the bold inquiring spirit of Aristotle and developing his beginnings to new conclusions, his followers killed the whole point of his work. It may be that the orthodox Freudians in our own time are doing the same to the creative writings of Freud – treating his views as axiomatic instead of as starting-points for new inquiries.

The genuinely creative thinker, on the other hand, is both critical of unsound views and yet adventurous in extending and developing new ideas. He is receptive towards what others have thought, although unwilling to accept it as final. He sifts out the sound parts from the unsound and attempts to develop and experiment with what satisfies the critic in him as worthy of attention. L. L. Thurstone, the author of *The Nature of Intelligence*, once distinguished between two types of student that he had met over the course of a long teaching career: X who is critical and analytical, and Y who is possessed of creative talent. Whenever X is confronted with a new hypothesis or novel proposal he tends to react by showing that it is absurd or unpractical: by clear, logical thinking which is often subtle and ingenious he analyses the suggestion away. Y, on the other hand, 'toys with it and speculates what the implications might be if they could be demonstrated. Because of the novelty of the proposal his impulse is to wish it could be shown to be true'. Both attitudes have their pitfalls. X, in spite of his cleverness at shaping well-turned arguments, may miss the point of an obscurely formulated but pregnant hypothesis: Y may, on occasion, prove gullible to superficially plausible but basically absurd notions. X may be intellectually docile – a diehard who preserves existing traditions even when they are ceasing to be relevant to changing circumstances (X is often acclaimed a great scholar) and Y may never settle down to the discipline of acquiring a reliable critical capacity.

Clearly Thurstone's common-sensical observation leads to the conclusion that a balance is required between critical capacity and receptivity. Nevertheless the emphasis in creative thinking is probably on the readiness to side with and explore sympathetically what possibilities are to be found in a new hypothesis, concept, or attitude. Excessive 'hypercriticism' of outlook or rigidity in sticking to conventional methods and concepts will block creativity – however intelligent and well educated the thinker may be.

Such attitudes are probably a function of what we mean, in ordinary language, by 'personality' – of that structure which psycho-analysts try to investigate and describe when dealing with abnormal subjects. This is obviously a vast area for the psychologist to explore and indicates yet another variable which determines 'how we think' on any given occasion.

MOTIVATIONAL FACTORS

Again, motivational factors obviously affect creativity. What drives X to train, qualify, and seek employment as a research physicist and Y to train and try to make a living as a writer? Each might be successful in many other walks of life – as administrators, politicians, lawyers – or might perhaps enjoy greater material and social benefits if they were to take a different course. Yet X and Y in some sense are 'involved' in their work and keep at it in spite of many difficulties and discouragements.

Many children of high I.Q. never exploit their ability: they drift into routine, unskilled jobs. Somehow the urge or drive to use their native talent is lacking or thwarted or turned sour. There is no guarantee, in any country where every facility is provided for any young person to obtain free education or training, that more than a handful of the youth of that country will be willing to submit to 'higher education'. If well-paid but unskilled jobs are readily available many may prefer to take the line of least resistance and earn a comfortable living without having to use their brains or develop their native capacities. Creative thinking is only possible for an individual who not only has the ability but the motivation to submit both to disciplined preparation and the self-discipline needed in all original work.

As we have already observed, psychologists know little about motivation, and yet it is an important determinant of all the activities we refer to when we use the concept of 'thought'.

BI-POLAR ACTIVITY

Finally, there must be a neat switching of 'gears' between the Imaginative pole (free flow of ideas – product of the unconscious function of the personality structure, determined by motivational state) and the Realistic pole (deliberate organization and control of data, application of skills and techniques: 'editing' one's own thought products, etc.). Creative thinking must involve the exercise of both intellect and imagination – to use the terminology of the old philosophy of mind.

IMAGINATION

The realistic pole is the one to which most of our attention has been drawn throughout the preceding chapters of this book: we have tended to consider 'thinking' in the special sense in which it is synonymous with 'reasoning' or 'reflecting logically'.

Imagination is, nevertheless, equally important. But what precisely do we mean by this concept? It is highly ambiguous and it is worth while spending some time in trying to clarify it.

As Ryle has argued, when a man is described as 'using his imagination' or 'thinking imaginatively' he may be doing any one of a number of quite different things. Ryle's examples illustrate his point with characteristic clarity and forcefulness. A witness in court inventing a plausible tale and the Judge weighing it up; an inventor working on a new machine and a colleague giving his opinion and advice on the blueprint; a writer spinning a romantic story and his readers following it; an actor performing in a play and his audience enjoying it – all these people are exercising their imagination. Inventing, acting, reading fiction, theatre-going, all these very different sorts of activity are classifiable as 'imagination-involving activities'.

Can we make any distinctions between the different uses of the concept of 'imagination'? Professor C. A. Mace, Professor of Psychology at London University, has done this job very thoroughly.* He distinguishes at least three quite different senses of the term.

PRACTICAL IMAGINATION

Many objects which are manufactured by human industry (women's hats and dresses, pieces of furniture, pottery) and also the products of artists (paintings, sculptures, musical compositions) are often praised by saying that they display 'imagination' on the part of their creators. Again actors, singers, ballet dancers, and other performers are credited with 'imaginative' displays. In each case there is a product or result which is observable or tangible and which demands ability, skill, and intelligence on the part of a human agent for its occurrence. Hence, to use 'imagination' in this context is to say something about the abilities, skills, etc., of the agent; it is to imply that they are perfected abilities – well developed and well applied.

* *Proceedings of the Aristotelian Society*, 1942–3: 'Concerning Imagination'.

LINGUISTIC IMAGINATION

The word 'imagination' is also employed when praising the work of poets, novelists, preachers, or orators who use words in speech or writing to stimulate a large audience. Again what is being talked about, when the word is used, is the skill of the word-users in achieving their objects through linguistic prowess. They are clever at mastering language.

REPRESENTATIONAL IMAGINATION

Sometimes we are said to exercise our imagination when we are visualizing, in the mind's eye, what is not present to the senses. We can imagine the home of our childhood or how Paris looked back in 1935. We can also imagine what we have never perceived in the past – the Tower of Babel, or how the garden would look if we dug up the grass and laid a crazy pavement instead.

This sort of imagining is not so important as some of the older psychologists used to think. There are all kinds of effective substitutes for visual, auditory, and other varieties of imagery. What one is imagining can be represented in words (spoken or written), in drawings made on paper or other surfaces, by humming or whistling or strumming on the piano. Imagery, which represents something other than itself, can be displaced by descriptions, sketches, models which serve the same purpose, do the same job.

There is a further stage, beyond the limits of 'imagination', in the senses distinguished by Mace and Ryle, which must be mentioned here. This is what psychologists call 'autistic thinking'. It takes such forms as fantasy, reverie, wishful thinking, day-dreaming. The associations which are formed in autistic thinking are regarded as being determined entirely by inner stimuli (needs, wishes, conflicts) as distinct from external stimuli. In imagination, the free play is evoked by specific external stimuli, by a definite problem or task, and there is thus a 'control' factor. In imagination the immediate demands of perceptual data are relaxed: the physical and social environment ceases to be central and the free play of association, the melting-pot in which the data of primary and secondary perception interact, takes over; all this takes place within the framework of a specific task or problem or need which, in a sense, is imposed from without. The distinction between problem-solving behaviour and imaginative exploration is vague and shifting. But there is a clearer distinction between problem-solving autistic thinking.

Nevertheless, almost any of these different kinds of activity may be involved in genuine creativity. 'Imagination' covers a host of different activities which have often little in common with each other, except that they are freer from the constraints of the external environment than many other psychological functions ('perception', 'learning', 'problem-solving'). 'Autistic thought' also covers a host of different activities from the harmless reverie of the shop assistant to the hallucinations of a psychotic patient in a mental hospital. In what ways then can 'imaginative' thinking serve as a source for creative thought products?

IMAGINATIVE AND OTHER 'FREE' ACTIVITIES AS A SOURCE

Many creative thinkers have placed on record the sources of their ideas.

Dreams. It sometimes happens that a key-concept occurs first in a dream. Descartes, the brilliant philosopher and mathematician, seems to have hit upon some of the axioms for his analytic geometry in a dream, while Kekulé, the chemist, evolved the concept of the benzene ring from the pictorial content of a dream.

Hypnagogic Imagery. This type of imagery may be visual, auditory, kinaesthetic, or of any other sense. It occurs in that drowsy, uncertain condition just before one falls into deep sleep. It was in such a state that Richard Wagner is supposed to have composed the haunting prelude to *Das Rheingold* and Lewis Carroll derived so much from this source that he invented a peculiar instrument, the 'nyctograph', to enable him to jot down ideas without fully waking up.

It is only one step from such normal imagery to hallucinations, drug-induced 'visions', and other 'abnormal' states. William Blake, poet and painter, is said to have painted certain of his famous visionary pictures while actually hallucinated. He seemed to see before him the angels and demons which he portrayed. Another example comes from an American mathematician who, having struggled vainly with a geometrical problem, woke up suddenly one morning and saw the solution on the wall of the bedroom, presented diagrammatically.

Eidetic Imagery. Some subjects are very vivid imagers. They can shut their eyes and clearly 'see in the mind's eye' a play or story enact itself as if being presented. The subject appears passive – as if in a cinema watching a film. Some imagers can continue to have this experience with open eyes. It is only after the material is written down that the subject recognizes that much of it is based on past experience – places visited, people met with, and incidents witnessed or read about are rearranged and developed to form the basis of an imagined tale. Sometimes bits of mathematical thinking appear to be aided by this semi-automatic combining and re-combining of ideas. Several authors of fiction appear to derive the bulk of their material from play with eidetic imagery.

Finally, ordinary perceptual situations may provide stimulation. An author will use her own house as the setting for a story or use an actual person as a character (Dr Watson in Conan Doyle's *Sherlock Holmes*). A painter may use a casual visitor to a church as the model for his Madonna ('Cavaradossi', using the Marchesa di Attevanti in *La Tosca*). Casual observations may suggest hypotheses (the myths of Archimedes in his bath, or Newton's apple, or Watt's kettle).

'Imagination' then may contribute to creativity in many different ways. Dreams, imagery of various kinds, and re-membered items from perceptual experiences may all be used as sources for new materials. Also 'imaginative' thinking in the sense of the skilful, adventurous, and individual use of one's skills, abilities, and talents in executing a particular task is clearly part of what is meant by 'creativity'. It is not so much the capacities but the manner in which they are applied which counts. What precisely 'imagination' involves in action is not easy to say. Mr Stephen Spender probably says as much as can be said when he tells us that creativity is 'to be what one is with all one's faculties and perceptions, strengthened by all the skill which one can acquire. ...' To act imaginatively is to be spontaneously honest in one's self-expression and to express oneself with taste and vigour.

CONCLUSION

It is obvious that we cannot explain what it is that makes for outstanding ability in creative work. We do not know enough about the human personality as a complete whole to be able to detect the factors which make for the differences between genius, outstanding performer, and ordinary 'average' ability. The judgement may be hazarded, however, that these differences, however great, are a matter of degree. There are several considerations which point in the direction of this view.

In the first place, identical discoveries and inventions have frequently been made independently and almost simultaneously by different thinkers (Leibniz and Newton with the calculus, Darwin and Wallace with the theory of evolution of species by natural selection). Even if a genius was needed to take the step, the time was ripe for it to be taken.

Again, however gifted, the outstanding man needs training and other favourable assistance in his work. Skills and techniques must be acquired and practised, and the help of other people is needed in order that the thinker should receive stimulation and direction. Darwin and Wallace both hit on their biological theory through reading an eighteenth-century treatise on economics (Malthus on 'Population'). Kant would never have thought seriously about publishing if he had not been shaken out of his 'dogmatic slumbers' by his equally great stimulator, David Hume: it was on reading Hume's *Enquiry* that Kant really became excited about certain philosophical problems.

Creative thinking is conditioned by many humdrum factors which influence the genius as much as the beginner. Most of us indulge in some genuine creative activity from time to time. The young woman who designs and makes herself a new hat or dress is thinking creatively. So is the young man who builds himself a radio set, or a schoolboy writing a letter home on his first trip abroad, or a young schoolmaster planning a lecture course for an adult class on 'the sociology of contemporary films'. The products in each case may be original, imaginative, vigorous. What distinguishes the great artist or thinker is his consistently high output of good work, his deeper sensitivity, his greater flexibility and adventurousness – and, of course, his superior training and 'education for life'. Yet the difference is probably one of degree. It may be that there is some factor, present in the case of the outstanding performer, which is absent in the case of the average creator and which accounts for his 'leap ahead' of normal learning, perceptual stimulation, personality traits. But if there is such a factor, we have no inkling as to what it might be.

When the time comes for an empirically grounded 'psychology of personality' we may be able to provide a more satisfying account of creative thinking. Personality factors are clearly of fundamental importance not merely in helping to define the limits of an individual's ability but also the special talents he develops and the style in which he engages in his characteristic pursuits.

'Personality' variables – whatever they may be – are yet another determinant of thought processes.

SELECTED REFERENCES

Ghiselin, B. *The Creative Process: A Symposium*. University of California Press, 1952.

Henri Poincaré. 'Mathematical Creation'.

Stephen Spender. 'The Making of a Poem'.

Dorothy Canfield. 'How "Flint and Fire" began to grow'.

Hall, C. S., and Lindzey, G. *Theories of Personality*. New York (Wiley), 1957.

Leeper, R. 'Congitive Processes'. Chapter 19 in S. S. Stevens, *A Handbook of Experimental Psychology*. New York (Wiley), 1951.

Mace, C. A. *The Psychology of Study*. London (Methuen), 1932.

McKeller, P. *Imagination and Thinking: A Psychological Analysis*. London (Cohen and West), 1957.

Montmasson, J.-M. *Invention and the Unconscious*. (Trans. H. Stafford Hatfield) London (Kegan Paul), 1931.

Murphy, G. *Human Potentialities*. New York (Basic Books), 1958.

Patrick, C. 'Creative Thought in Poets'. *Arch. Psychology*, 1935, No. 178.

Patrick, C. 'Creative Thought in Artists'. *Journal of Psychology*, 1937.

Patrick, C. *What is Creative Thinking?* New York (Philosophical Library), 1955.

Vinacke, W. E. *The Psychology of Thinking*. Chapter 12, New York (McGraw-Hill), 1952.

CHAPTER ELEVEN

What do we know about Thinking?

THIS discussion has been somewhat piecemeal, a presentation of bits and pieces of information together with an isolated and tentative hypothesis. This reflects the present state of our knowledge about thinking. Yet the situation is preferable to one in which a neat and consistent account is confidently put forward and which, once it is submitted to scrutiny, turns out to be mistaken.

A century ago psychologists were far more confident when discussing the nature of thought. Any text-book written in English during the 1850s would have presented some version or other of the then dominant Associationist Psychology. According to this theory, all psychological data could be analysed into simple elements; either sensations (the immediate product of sensory stimulation) or ideas (images derived from sensations). In thinking, ideas were supposed to be combined into complexes according to certain laws of association. These laws were derived from such principles as the regular coming together, in place and time, of two or more ideas, or through two separate ideas happening to resemble each other closely. The associationists were not agreed about the precise nature of this 'mental chemistry' but the general principle was clear: namely, that in order to describe and explain thinking all that was necessary was for the psychologist to introspect his own states of mind and to analyse the complex state to be found by this process into simple associated elements. The main task for psychology was to discover how exactly the components in such configurations were related to each other by the laws of association of ideas.

This simple theory has not merely been abandoned. It is realized by present-day psychologists that any all-inclusive theory which seeks to explain a wide range of behaviour in terms of a few simple principles is unsound. Why this is the case will emerge from what follows.

During the past eighty years, the short period during which psychology has been an independent discipline, there has been some progress in our understanding of the nature of thought. Indeed, we ought to be able to know what happens when we think, at least in general terms. The first step in any empirical inquiry is the collection and classification of the sorts of activity in which the researcher happens to be interested. The reason why the job of describing and classifying what sort of things we do when we think has been slow to get under way is that psychologists have been misled by certain metaphysical views about the human mind.

Much recent progress has resulted directly from the rejection of misleading philosophical theories or assumptions by psychologists. The change, in general, has been away from attempts to introspect and analyse the contents of individual consciousness and towards the attempt to study the operations of thinking behaviourally. What is essential in thinking can sometimes be rendered objective in the form of observable operations on the part of the subject. Failing this, what moves and counter-moves a thinker makes can be attacked indirectly by encouraging a situation in which overt clues bear a close relationship to covert activities.

The writings of Ryle are both a source and an exemplification of this change. Ryle has indicated at least three shifts in the approach to the study of thinking.

In the first place Ryle has argued that psychologists have been misled by certain associationist doctrines. In the early days of experimental psychology, psychologists tried to investigate thinking by looking for the precise connexions between images entertained by their subjects. Although imagery does occur in some thought processes those early investigators soon discovered enormous gaps between isolated bits of imagery and realized that images are not the stuff of which thinking consists. They next considered the hypothesis that judgements or mental acts were the crucial stages in a thought process. Again experiments revealed that such events are illusive and even illusory. Indeed, the search for such simple elements out of which thought processes are constructed was a mistake. As Ryle has argued the concept of thinking does not refer to the recurrence of specific content such as 'ideas' or 'acts' which are the materials, so to speak, which constitute the stuff of every piece of thinking. The concept refers to any one of a number of quite different sorts of activity. The realization that the older psychologists were misconstruing the concept of 'thought' and failing to understand what 'thinking' means, has led modern psychologists to abandon the attempt to analyse states of consciousness into mental elements. Instead they attempt to study what sort of things a thinker does, what types of behaviour occur, and under what general conditions, and with what results when he is properly describable as 'thinking'.

Secondly, Ryle has suggested that thinking is partly to be regarded as a complex of 'drills and skills'. Learning and training are an integral part of such intelligent behaviour. In some cases there is no need to look for further ingredients beyond such drills and skills and their manner of being exercised. Thus learning and the performance of what has been learned are crucial in the description and explanation of thought processes. Psychologists have also come to this conclusion. The study of thought is closely related to the study of learning. Indeed, thinking is often regarded as the ultimate point on a continuum which begins with habits and conditioning and ends with intelligent insight.

Finally, Ryle has attacked the metaphysical dualism which made such a drastic distinction between mind and body, between consciousness and physical activity. Ryle has argued that mental happenings can be adequately described and interpreted in behavioural terms. How this concept of behaviour is to be analysed in order to include both covert and overt responses presents some difficulties. Nevertheless both philosophers and psychologists believe that a working analysis can be provided which serves their general purposes when thinking about thought better than did the old mentalistic model of sensations and ideas.

The result of this change has been for psychologists to ask, 'What sort of things does a person actually *do* when thinking?' And having answered the question, the next step is to devise methods of objectifying what a person does who thinks so that they may be subjected to controlled study. Much of the previous chapters of this book have been concerned with attempts on the part of psychologists to render the crucial activities in thought sufficiently overt to be noted and described with some accuracy. We have seen how Piaget attempted to objectify the operations of classifying, serializing, and enumerating, and the methods in terms of which such operations are organized and integrated. Also, in the experiments of Bruner and his associates, we saw how the concept of specific strategies enabled the experimenters to describe how concrete operations are organized into patterns to achieve the results demanded in a concept-attainment task. These studies are merely a beginning at the task of objectifying thought processes and studying them experimentally. But they do succeed in showing what specific operations are tried out by each subject and how his specific actions are coordinated into sequences of directed behaviour to attain specific results. Only limited types of situation have been investigated so far. But others, which have not been studied yet or may not even have been discovered, may be amenable to treatment along similar lines.

The facts available at present, as the result of experimental studies, are scanty; but this can be remedied. Only a limited amount of work has been done on thought since Wundt opened the first psychology laboratory in 1879. What is needed is much more empirical data. However, we know the kind of information to be obtained even if the searching has so far been done on too limited a scale. Thus the materials are beginning to be assembled out of which a descriptive psychology of thinking may be built gradually. Partly as a result of our general knowledge about our own and other people's thinking, partly as a result of an analysis of the concepts used to refer to thinking in everyday speech, and partly as a result of experimental studies, we must categorize the different types of situation to which the concept of 'thought' applies. This is the first step in any empirical science and it is not yet completed for the psychology of thinking.

It is necessary to keep in mind the fact that 'thinking' is a polymorphous concept which applies to a considerable range of different sorts of activity. Whether or not these different types of activity are related to each other, and, if so, in what specific ways, is a question which must be always kept in view. When a person is thinking, it is usually the case that several of these distinguishable sorts of activity are involved within the same situation – visual and other types of imagery; verbal contents; insights; performances which are the result of the evocation of prior learning; strugglings which are the steps towards the acquisition of new skills or concepts; goal-directed behaviour which conforms to well-established rule-following models and goal-directed behaviour which is exploratory in the means it adopts towards what may be an unfamiliar goal; operations which conform to strategies of a strictly logical form and leaps in the dark which appear unrelated to any other part of a long series of activities. Since a particular thought session may exhibit such a variety of activity perhaps there is some point in looking for connexions between different categories of thought. However, this is a task of considerable difficulty and it is wise first to try to isolate and investigate separately each recognizable type of activity.

Moreover, the study of thinking is dependent upon progress in other fields of psychological research. It has been emphasized that thinking is sometimes essentially learning or performance; the thinker is either striving to attain a new capacity or concept or skill or else is executing a skilful performance in virtue of previous learning and training. Yet learning theory is still in a formative phase of development and is likely to remain so for many years. It is only since the First World War that learning operations have been studied extensively by psychologists and there are still many points of controversy and uncertainty to be cleared up before any substantial progress can be expected. Furthermore, psychologists have confined their attention to the simplest forms of learning (viz. conditioning) and are not in a position to interpret the more complex learning which is characteristic of thought processes. Until more is known about the psychology of learning the study of thought must remain correspondingly immature.

Apart from the speculations of Freud, Jung, Adler, and other psycho-therapists, the whole field of motivation is still largely unexplored territory. There has been a good deal of confused thinking about motivation on the part of psychologists and hardly any empirical investigations have been carried out into the relation between motivated behaviour and learning and performance. Thinking is among the most purposive of all varieties of behaviour and is therefore intimately related to the study of motives. If we wish to explain a particular bit of behaviour, which is describable as 'thought', it is probable that reference to the subject's motives and needs may provide the explanation we are seeking. Yet until the psychology of motivation has advanced considerably beyond its present speculative phase, few sound explanations of thought processes can be given.

The achievements or limitations of a thinker in a specific situation are clearly influenced by a wide range of variables. The system of habits and skills involved in using language is crucial for the character of thought processes, and yet the psychological study of language is still in its most primitive stage; the processes of imaginative thought, particularly in relation to the problem of what assists originality or creativity, are still largely uninvestigated. The study of the manner in which thought is circumscribed by the personality of the individual thinker is yet another partly developed, but still uncertain, field of relevant interest. Until progress, in such broad areas of psychology, goes far beyond the present level of achievement, the psychology of thinking will remain a somewhat bare and tentative affair. However, it may be claimed that the areas to be explored have been mapped in outline and that there is a reasonable hope that with time and effort our knowledge will be greatly increased.

One final uncertainty remains. It is only eighty years, at the time of writing, since the metaphysical approach to psychological questions was abandoned in favour of a strictly empirical approach. Psychologists are not yet certain whether the methods and presuppositions in terms of which their investigations are carried out are the most appropriate ones to use when studying behaviour empirically. Many different models and techniques have been tried out in the course of the past eighty years, but, so far, no fundamental agreement has been reached. At present the methods employed are neither sufficiently like those of physics or physiology to satisfy those who demand that psychology must be a natural science (no more and no less!) nor sufficiently flexible to satisfy others who consider that psychologists must devise methods more suited to the data (viz. more like the methods of anthropology and sociology). The Freudians and other derivative schools advocate their own distinctive approach to make the division of opinion still more acute, and there does not seem to be any likelihood of an early resolution of the methodological problem. At any rate, all the conventional methods are in a trial and error phase of development – laboratory experiments, field work, data from the clinic, interview and questionnaire techniques, psychometric tests and sociological surveys. All require further refinement and adaptation before the intractable-seeming data of human and animal behaviour can be described and explained with the subtlety it demands. In this situation it is the study of the higher functions which suffers most; hence the psychology of thinking remains a field of piecemeal investigations none of which has reached an advanced stage of development; as such it must be presented and accepted.

CONCLUSION

Although thinking has been a topic for scrutiny since the time of Plato and Aristotle, we still have a long road to travel before our knowledge is anything better than speculative.

The Psychology of Thinking

At present psychologists regard thinking as a heterogeneous collection of high-level skills and capacities which result from the coordination and integration of many simpler functions. These lower-level activities are organized in terms of the sort of operations which are studied in the psychology of learning and the psychology of motivation and are modified by a host of variable factors. To explain how the high-level activities are developed from simpler activities is probably the main task for the psychology of thinking in the immediate future.

This task can only be undertaken through a large number of separate investigations, each concerned with a highly specific situation in which one type of skill or group of skills is isolated for thorough scrutiny. Thus it is unwise to attempt to define the scope of the psychology of thinking in advance. Any definition would limit the field unduly. For example, the traditional nineteenth-century definition of thought, for the purposes of psychology, was 'an associated train of ideas'. This fits certain kinds of thinking but not others. Again to define thought as categorizing on the basis of readily discriminable cues fits some cases but not others. The most popular definition of thinking, in recent years, has been Dewey's characterization of thought as problem-solving behaviour. Against this, too, objections can be raised. Dewey's conception emphasizes that thought may have grown out of man's need to adapt himself to a difficult and often hostile environment. Throughout life, especially in simple communities, needs have to be adjusted to events beyond the immediate control of the subject. At the same time the subject can change certain factors in his environment in order to forestall or limit future difficulties and dangers. Thought has thus developed as an instrument for controlling and mastering a difficult environment. Thinking was originally a weapon in man's armoury for defence and attack in the struggle for survival. Once the environment has been partly tamed thought has become capable of various refinements and can be indulged in spontaneously for its own sake and not merely in situations in which an individual is forced to think. Yet Dewey's definition has led psychologists to over-stress the practical, adaptive character of much thinking. When the experimental psychologist observes him the thinker is often strenuously engaged with some tough problem which involves struggle and effort. Thinking is an activity, of course, and the thinker has to have all the qualities of a 'man of action'. But we often think of a thinker, not as a wrestler with difficulties thrust upon him, but as a contemplative who detaches himself from struggling with the world and who stands back to consider it abstractly in a cool hour. Moreover, however one defines 'problem-solving' there will always be cases which are instances of a man thinking but which do not comply with our criteria for 'problem-solving behaviour'. Asking and answering questions, explaining the occurrence of a particular event, or analysing a concept of proposition – all these are instances of thinking but they might not fit the pattern of problem-solving behaviour in which the thinker is stirred into action by the appearance of a disturbance or challenge which upsets his equilibrium and forces him to deal with it.

No simple definition or analysis exhibits what is common to the large variety of situations in which a person is properly described as thinking, even if we confine the concept to the use in which it means 'reasoning' or 'reflective thinking'. Each type of situation has to be investigated separately and related to the others only if connexions are revealed.

There are many questions about thinking and many approaches which have not been discussed in this book. If we wanted to discover some of the necessary conditions of thought and to explain certain breakdowns in the capacity of a thinker to think efficiently, we would have to consider the physiology of the brain and nervous system. Deviations from normal thinking are discussed by psychiatrists and psycho-therapists, and their studies in abnormal thinking throw light, if only by comparison, on normal thought processes. The factors studied by psychologists interested in intelligence tests throw light on the extent to which, and the ways in which, individual differences occur in thinking; they provide us with a rough and ready measure of the difference between average and outstanding abilities. Social psychologists study the influence of social relationships within a given social group upon the style and content of individual thinking. There are even interesting analogies between *some* aspects of human thinking and the achievements of electronic artefacts which work out logical problems. All these different specialists ask different questions about thinking and have to supply appropriate answers by employing approaches which differ according to the question and its requirements. Each contributes another dimension to our understanding of thought processes. In this book we have confined ourselves to a discussion of the task of creating a descriptive psychology of individual thought processes by adapting the methods of Experimental Psychology.

This task is far from being completed. And yet, considering the small amount of time and effort given to it so far, its progress has not been unsatisfactory. This branch of psychology deserves encouragement. Not only is thinking a topic of considerable intrinsic interest, but its study may have some practical importance. The application of genuine knowledge concerning thought processes to education, mental health, and social problems may yet make a major contribution to human welfare.

SELECTED REFERENCES

Bartlett, F. C. *Thinking*. London (Allen and Unwin), 1958.
Boring, E. G. *A History of Experimental Psychology*. New York (Appleton-Century-Crofts), 1950.
Dewey, J. *How We Think*. New York (D. C. Heath), 1933.
Hearnshaw, L. S. 'Recent Studies in the Psychology of Thinking.' *The Advancement of Science*, No. 42, September 1954.
Ryle, G. 'Thinking.' *Acta Psychologica*, 1953.
Sluckin, W. *Minds and Machines*. Pelican Books, 1954.

ADDITIONAL REFERENCES

CHAPTER 3 (p. 62)

Gagne, R. M. 'Problem Solving and Thinking'. *Annual Review of Psychology*, 10, 1959.

Maier, N. R. F. 'Reasoning in Humans' (I to IV), in *Journal of Comparative Psychology*, 1930 and 1931; *Psychological Review*, 1940; and *Journal of Experimental Psychology*, 1945.

Ruger, H. 'The Psychology of Efficiency'. *Archives of Psychology*, 1910.

Taylor, D. W., and McNemar, O. W. 'Problem Solving and Thinking'. *Annual Review of Psychology*, 6, 1955.

CHAPTER 6 (p. 132)

Ruch, F. L. 'Adult Learning'. *Psychological Bulletin*, 1933.

Welford, A. T. *Ageing and Human Skill*. London (Oxford University Press), 1958.

MORE ABOUT PENGUINS
AND PELICANS

If you have enjoyed reading this book you may wish to know that *Penguin Book News* appears every month. It is an attractively illustrated magazine containing a complete list of books published by Penguins and still in print, together with details of the month's new books. A specimen copy will be sent free on request.

Penguin Book News is obtainable from most bookshops; but you may prefer to become a regular subscriber at 3s. for twelve issues. Just write to Dept EP, Penguin Books Ltd, Harmondsworth, Middlesex, enclosing a cheque or postal order, and you will be put on the mailing list.

Some other books published by Penguins are described on the following pages.

Note: *Penguin Book News* is not
available in the U.S.A.,
Canada or Australia

FREUD AND THE POST-FREUDIANS

J. A. C. Brown

Freud and the Post-Freudians explains the main concepts of Freudian psychology and goes on to review the theories of Adler, Jung, Rank, and Stekel. Later developments in the orthodox Freudian school are also discussed, as are those of the American Neo-Freudians and Post-Freudians in England.

This is the first book published in Britain to bring together all these psychological and sociological schools and criticize them, both from the Freudian standpoint and that of the scientific psychologists.

THE SOCIAL PSYCHOLOGY OF INDUSTRY

J. A. C. Brown

In recent years it has become increasingly apparent that the classical approach to industrial psychology is inadequate. This approach regarded the worker primarily as a machine to be studied by the techniques of physiological psychology and as an isolated individual whose aptitudes caused him to be suited or unsuited for a given job. The results obtained by such an approach are not necessarily wrong, but, as Elton Mayo demonstrated conclusively more than twenty years ago, they are bound to be incomplete because the ' isolated ' human being is a fiction. Since each individual is a member of society and each worker a member of a working group, the attitudes of these groups are bound to play a large part in influencing his behaviour both as citizen and worker. The author has tried to discuss such fundamental questions as: what is human nature? what causes men to work? what is morale? and what influence has the nature of industrial work upon the mental health of the individual worker and his community?

Also available

TECHNIQUES OF PERSUASION

PSYCHOLOGY IN PELICANS

Pelican books have achieved an enviable reputation for publishing first-class books in psychology for the general reader. Among the titles available are:

CHILDHOOD AND ADOLESCENCE
J. A. Hadfield

FREUD AND THE POST-FREUDIANS
J. A. C. Brown

KNOW YOUR OWN I.Q.
H. J. Eysenck

THE NORMAL CHILD
and Some of his Abnormalities
C. W. Valentine

INTRODUCTION TO JUNG'S PSYCHOLOGY
Frieda Fordham

THE PSYCHOLOGY OF PERCEPTION
M. D. Vernon

SENSE AND NONSENSE IN PSYCHOLOGY
H. J. Eysenck

USES AND ABUSES OF PSYCHOLOGY
H. J. Eysenck

FACT AND FICTION IN PSYCHOLOGY
H. J. Eysenck

A DICTIONARY OF PSYCHOLOGY
James Drever

MORE PSYCHOLOGY IN PELICANS

Among the other books on psychology published in Pelicans are:

CHILD CARE AND THE GROWTH OF LOVE
John Bowlby and Margaret Fry

HUMAN GROUPS
W. J. K. Sprott

MEMORY
Ian M. L. Hunter

PSYCHIATRY TODAY
David Stafford-Clark

THE PSYCHOLOGY OF SEX
Oswald Schwarz

THE PSYCHOLOGY OF STUDY
C. A. Mace

FUNDAMENTALS OF PSYCHOLOGY
C. J. Adcock

THE SOCIAL PSYCHOLOGY OF INDUSTRY
J. A. C. Brown

Also available in Penguins:

THE CHILD'S WORLD
Phyllis Hostler

USES AND ABUSES OF PSYCHOLOGY

H. J. Eysenck

Psychology occupies a somewhat ambiguous place in the world today. Its findings are being widely applied in clinics, in industry, in education, and in the armed forces. At the same time, many intelligent people are critical of the alleged laws of human behaviour discovered by psychologists, psychiatrists, and psychoanalysts, and doubtful about the applicability of scientific methods to the study of human beings. In this book, a well-known psychologist has tried to strike a balance, to indicate to what extent the claims made for his science are justified, and to what extent they fail to have any factual basis. The discussion is very fully documented by references to the most important and relevant researches carried out in this country and abroad. Topics dealt with are the testing of intelligence, selection procedures in schools and universities, vocational guidance and occupational selection, psychotherapy and its effects, national differences, racial intolerance, Gallup surveys, industrial productivity, and many others. In each case, psychological findings are submitted to a searching criticism, and a clear distinction made between those uses of psychology where enough is known to support social action, and those abuses where personal opinions rather than experimentally demonstrated fact seem to be involved.

SENSE AND NONSENSE
IN PSYCHOLOGY

H. J. Eysenck

There are many topics in modern psychology about which speculation has been rife for hundreds of years. Much has been written on the powers and dangers of the hypnotic trance, the wonders of telepathy and clairvoyance, the possibility of the interpretation of dreams, the nature and assessment of personality, and the psychology of beauty. These early views, while often amusing, have little value because they are not based on scientific facts. In recent years, much experimental evidence has been collected regarding all these topics, but few reliable accounts have appeared which would acquaint the interested layman with these facts and their possible interpretations and implications. This is what the author has attempted to do in this book, carefully reviewing and sifting the evidence, by boldly putting forward a definite point of view where the evidence appears to justify it. Throughout the book emphasis is laid particularly on the detailed discussion of the facts, leaving to the reader the decision as to whether the conclusions drawn are justified.

KNOW YOUR OWN I.Q.

H. J. Eysenck

Intelligence Quotient, as a useful means of measuring brain capacity, has come more and more into the public eye in recent years.

This is at present the only book which permits the reader to determine his own I.Q. In the first part of it the well-known author of *Sense and Nonsense in Psychology, Uses and Abuses of Psychology* and *Fact and Fiction in Psychology* describes clearly what an I.Q. is, how it can be applied, and what the shortcomings of this system of rating may be.

The second part of the book contains eight sets of forty I.Q. problems each, and these are graduated from 'quite easy' to 'very difficult'. There are tables for converting results into an I.Q. rating, and also explanations of the problems, together with the right answers, at the end of the book.